COUPON
CRAZY

COUPON
CRAZY

THE SCIENCE,

THE SAVINGS,

& THE STORIES

BEHIND

AMERICA'S

EXTREME

Obsession

MARY POTTER KENYON

Published by Familius LLC, www.familius.com

Familius books are available at special discounts for bulk purchases for sales promotions, family or corporate use. Special editions, including personalized covers, excerpts of existing books, or books with corporate logos, can be created in large quantities for special needs. For more information, contact Premium Sales at 559-876-2170 or email special-markets@familius.com

Library of Congress Catalog-in-Publication Data

2013941696

pISBN 978-1-938301-88-9
eISBN 978-1-938301-89-6

Printed in the United States of America

Edited by Maggie Wickes and Anji Sandage
Cover Design by David Miles
Book Design by Maggie Wickes and David Miles
Back Cover Photo by Daniel Kenyon
All coupons used in this book come from the personal collection of Mary Potter Kenyon.

10 9 8 7 6 5 4 3 2 1

First Edition

Contents

I would like to dedicate this book to the mother who was my artistic muse, Irma Potter, and the husband who became the wind beneath my wings, David Edward Kenyon. David, you always believed in me. This book was originally your idea, and I couldn't have done it without you, and yet, in the end, I had to. To my beautiful grandson, Jacob, who has bravely fought a childhood cancer during the two years I've worked on this manuscript. And to my eight children who lived the sometimes crazy lifestyle of an avid couponer and refunder and supported me throughout this endeavor: Daniel, Elizabeth, Michael, Rachel, Matthew, Emily, Katherine, and Abigail.

I love all of you.

Endorsements

"You'll never understand couponing until you've read *Coupon Crazy*.

"As Mary Kenyon points out, in spite of the current furor over social media darling, Groupon and its hundreds of imitators, the use of coupons by manufacturers and retailers has been around since the late nineteenth century.

"Nielson categorizes people who use 104 coupons in a 26 week period as a "Coupon Enthusiast," and as Mary confesses she uses at least that many in a week, so she is more than justified as describing herself as an "Extreme Couponer."

"When it comes to coupons, the companies and businesses that issue them, and the people who clip, save, scavenge, and use them, Mary certainly knows her stuff.

"This is not just a book that is meticulously researched and full of information of value to any marketer who wishes to truly understand what a successful couponing program can achieve by stepping outside the dry nuts and bolts of data analysis, this is a book written by someone who isn't ashamed to talk about how she and her kids used to go dumpster diving for proof of purchase and redemption tags from discarded packages.

"There are tens of thousands of "Coupon Enthusiasts" out there, it is critically important for marketers to understand what motivates them and how to incentivize them to progress from one-off opportunists to repeat customers.

"*Coupon Crazy* shows you how to do this. It's also a fun read."

George Parker

George Parker has spent more than 40 years on Madison Avenue. He's won Lions, CLIOs, EFFIES, and the David Ogilvy Award. His blog is adscam.typepad.com, which he describes as, "required reading for those looking for a piss & vinegar view of the world's second oldest profession." His latest book, Confessions of a Mad Man, *makes the TV show* Mad Men *look like* Sesame Street.

"The saving money phenomenon is one of the most powerful consumer trends we have ever seen. Coupon Crazy goes beyond the headlines and television shows to unearth what this trend is all about, who it effects and why and underscores why it is here to stay. Every marketer, retailer and consumer needs to read this book, it offers the lessons to succeed both professionally and personally."

Phil Lempert, Editor, Columnist & CEO, www.SupermarketGuru.com

"Coupon Crazy" is a must read for any retailer or marketer in today's compulsively frugal world. Mary Potter Kenyon knows her subject cold and her compelling book will not only help your business get coupon savvy, her tips will save you a bundle in your personal life. A coupon manifesto that comes with its own built in bonus!"

Mary Lou Quinlan, Founder, *Just Ask a Woman,*
author, What She's Not Telling You

Foreword

BY JILL CATALDO

My passion for couponing began innocently enough. Like most people, I used coupons occasionally, clipping a few from the Sunday paper and trying to save a few dollars here and there. My transformation from casual coupon user to consumer coupon expert could quite possibly be traced to a single tube of toothpaste.

When I was pregnant with our third child, I became driven to save more money. I started paying closer attention to sales cycles at stores, and one week I noticed that toothpaste was on sale for a dollar. I happened to have a coupon for a dollar off the toothpaste, and the coupon made the toothpaste free.

All couponers have had their own "light bulb" moment—the first deal that begins a shift in the way you look at shopping and saving. Mary Potter Kenyon's moment just came a little earlier than most. As you will read in *Coupon Crazy*, she was ten years old when she sat at the kitchen table reading the back of a cereal box and realized she wanted to be one of those people who got things free. For me, that single tube of toothpaste was my epiphany. And from that moment forward, I became a better, smarter, and more strategic shopper. Matching coupons to sales and taking products home at the lowest possible prices was fun—almost addicting—and I reveled in the money that I was saving. Soon, I was teaching others to save via live workshops, a blog, and a nationally-syndicated column.

I've always enjoyed sharing my passion for couponing with anyone interested to learn, and in the current economy, interest in couponing remains high. People are looking to save money in every possible way, and when budgets are tight, coupons help families stretch their dollars in an easy, and often fun,way.

In the years I've been a serious couponer, I've seen many changes in the couponing world, changes that Mary discusses in *Coupon Crazy*. Paper coupons continue to top redemption rates among consumers each year, but print-at-home and electronic coupons continue to grow in popularity too. Additionally, online tools for couponers have exploded over the past decade. Grocery list "matchup" sites appeared online, tracking the lowest sale prices and matching coupons to sales. Then, between 2008 and 2010, coupon blogs exploded in popularity. Blogs offered localized deals and coupon instruction for beginners with step-by-step, easy-to-understand tips for chasing the sales and getting rock-bottom prices on everything from cereal to shampoo. To this day, thousands of bloggers around the country continue to share daily and weekly coupon deals with their readers.

In 2011, the TLC series *Extreme Couponing* thrust the concept of over-the-top coupon savings into the public eye on a weekly basis. Despite the show's often unrealistic portrayals of coupon usage, it piqued many people's interest in couponing, inspiring shoppers around the country to pick up a pair of scissors for the first time. Unfortunately, the show also featured extremists showing various ways to beat and cheat the system with coupons. Not content with the already-admirable savings that legitimate coupon use provided, some shoppers featured on the show even resorted to using counterfeit coupons, sending their savings soaring into the impossible-to-duplicate realm, with cartloads of ill-gotten, "free" groceries in tow.

In 2012, an enormous counterfeit coupon ring out of Phoenix was busted by authorities. The counterfeiters had made millions of dollars selling phony free-product coupons online—likely to some of the *Extreme Couponing* shoppers, as well as shoppers attempting to recreate some of the savings levels depicted on TV.

In the post-*Extreme-Couponing* world, we saw manufacturers respond with additional restrictions on coupons—everything from "Limit 4 Like Coupons Per Transaction" to "Limit One Per Customer." What other changes will the future hold for couponing? Time will tell. But I'll be waiting—scissors in hand.

Jill Cataldo

The register slowly spit out the receipt, a quarter inch at a time, calculating the tax and the coupon savings that fills the bottom half of the cash register tape. The cashier announces the final tally and I hear a gasp of surprise from the woman behind me, who'd been rolling her eyes at the delay just a moment before.

Total before coupons: $230. After coupons: $38. I'd combined high-value store coupons with manufacturer coupons so that most of the merchandise in my cart was free. The cashier carefully folded the receipt, smiling as she handed it to me. "Great shopping. You saved almost $200."

"That's what I do," I replied, thanking her for her patience. Then I turned around and handed the customer behind me a stack of coupons for the products she was buying, coupons I'd pulled from my coupon box after some surreptitious glances at her cart.

This is what I do, what I've been doing for more than thirty years.

My question: Why doesn't everyone?

Learn the Language

B1G1F or BOGO: Buy one item, get one free

Blinkie: A coupon pulled from the small red coupon dispenser attached to the grocery store shelf.

CAT, Catalina: A manufacturer coupon that prints out of a machine at the register, triggered by what you buy. Also known as "register rewards."

Cpn, c/o, c: Coupon, cents-off coupon

Complete Deal: A refund form with all the proofs (including cash register tapes) needed in order to send the form in for a refund. This was the term used in trading ads from the 80s and 90s.

CRT: Cash register tape

DCRT: Dated cash register tape

ECB: Extra Care Bucks, a register reward available at CVS

FAR: Free after rebate

NED: No expiration date (Popular for coupons from the past, rare today.)

OOP: Out of pocket, the expense of a deal after coupons are applied

MIR: Mail-in rebate

Peelies: Coupons that are attached to the product

POP: Proof of purchase, usually the UPC (Universal Product Code), but whatever is required to get a refund. Also called a "qualifier."

Q: Qualifier, same as proof of purchase above. Can also mean "coupon" on some chat boards, but to long-time couponers, it was always a qualifier or proof of purchase needed to complete a refund offer.

RR: Register Reward, the Catalina coupon at Walgreens

SMP: Specially marked package, with either a refund form, coupon, or special proof of purchase token printed right on the package.

Tear Pad: A block of coupons from which you tear an individual coupon.

UPC: Universal Product Code. Black lines with numbers that the checker passes over the scanner at a checkout. Each product has a unique code.

The Making of a Coupon Commando

"One. Two. Three. Four," Elizabeth counted out loud as she tossed the deodorants into the shopping cart. They landed with a satisfying *thunk* in the bottom. "How many more coupons do we have?"

A nearby customer couldn't help but smile at the unbridled enthusiasm of my teenage daughter. For an hour, Elizabeth and I had roamed the aisles of the Venture discount store, matching up coupons with our purchases and leaving the store with 150 dollars worth of merchandise for less than 25 dollars. The store was our battlefront, and we were prepared to fight inflation. We'd entered the store armed with a carefully organized coupon box and the motto "cheap is good, but free is better." I often used our shopping sprees as real-life math lessons in our homeschooling, but Elizabeth seemed to enjoy the hunt for good deals nearly as much as I did.

That was in the late 1990s, when coupons regularly saved me 30 to 50 percent off my grocery bill and manufacturer refunds easily netted me 100 dollars a month and the majority of my family's Christmas gifts. Shopping was like a big game, with me hunting to fill our cupboards with cheap or free soap and cereal and opening the mailbox every day to find it stuffed with rebate checks, free product coupons, and refund premiums. The Sunday newspaper, with the thick, glossy coupon inserts, was our key to savings. We'd been informed by a friendly worker at the recycling center that, because of their shiny texture, this section was often separated from the rest and discarded. He encouraged us to take as many coupon inserts as we wanted whenever we brought our own recycling to their bins.

We didn't need to be told twice. In those days, our family visited the recycling center several times a week, filling the back end of our old station wagon with coupon inserts along with the medicine boxes and empty laundry detergent jugs I needed for refunding. We'd pour hot water in the jugs and soak them in the bathtub until the labels slid right off, then return them to the recycling center on our next trip, when we'd pick up more. The labels were dried on paper towels on my kitchen counter, attached to index cards, and then filed in a large cabinet, along with pain reliever, antacid, make-up, and toothpaste boxes. I saved everything. Plastic sandwich bags held Kool-Aid points, battery UPC's, and candy bar wrappers. Long white envelopes filled with cereal box tops and bottoms were rubber-banded together. Trash meant cash back then, and the savvy refunder saved all of it in anticipation for future offers. I had an entire room devoted to my hobby, with a huge shelf and two filing cabinets. For serious couponers of this era, couponing was synonymous with refunding. It was about way more than just saving money at the grocery store; it was also about making money with manufacturer's refunds and providing unique premium gifts for family and friends. Double coupon opportunities allowed me to stock our shelves and cupboards with many free products. Thanks to stores like Venture and Food-4-Less, both now defunct in Iowa, I never paid more than a few pennies for basics like shampoo, toothpaste, or bandages. On Christmas morning, our cash-strapped family enjoyed a bounty of gifts that included T-shirts emblazoned with the Energizer Bunny, Jolly Green Giant, or the Hershey candy bar logo; stuffed animals; radios; hats; and one Christmas, a Little Tykes dollhouse that was totally free thanks to Luvs diaper proofs of purchase. Stockings were filled with Kraft Macaroni and Cheese, crayons, Flintstone and Ducktails character figurines, and foot-long pencils inscribed with the recipient's name. One year, a cigarette company offered televisions, radios, a video camera, and even a pool table, throwing avid refunders into a smoking and trading frenzy.

Back then, refund and rebate offers were plentiful, ranging from Crest-sponsored AT&T gift certificates that paid my phone bills for several months, to a free coffeemaker from Folgers and strings of M&M Christmas lights. The majority of offers were unlimited and didn't require cash register receipts, accounting for the aforementioned files that bulged with empty bags and boxes. When an offer came out, all I had to do was go to my files and pull out the proofs of purchase needed to fulfill them. I didn't stop there. I was not above filching empty candy bar wrappers from trash bins at the park or picking up the back cards of batteries from store parking lots. My children all sported Hershey shirts but ate very few of the required candy bars themselves to get them. Trips to the pool were the most rewarding, where candy was sold at the concession stand and the trash receptacles were overflowing with wrappers. On neighborhood trash day, the children and I walked up and down the alleys, where we confiscated extra Pampers points to send in for savings bonds and toys. Even the tennis shoes my children wore on these jaunts were obtained free from the Huggies diaper company.

In 1991 I thought I'd died and gone to heaven when a former neighbor called and asked me if I wanted her deceased husband's stash of proofs of purchase and qualifiers that filled an entire basement. Whatever I didn't want, she would be throwing out. I passed over complete cereal boxes from the 70s in favor of the more recent qualifiers. Much later I would regret that move when I got online and saw collectors of cereal boxes paid top dollar for those same boxes, flattened or not.

In the 80s and 90s, magazines devoted to refunding and couponing were prolific, offering support and trading opportunities for people like me, the avid coupon users and refunders. At one point, I was trading with fourteen other women through the mail, each of us filling an envelope for the other from their wish list of coupons and refund forms. We all loved saving money through our hobby. We were, and are, a different breed of shopper, one

> "Vintage cereal boxes, particularly from the 50s, 60s, and 70s, have become highly collectible, selling for as much as $200 or $300. Early packages of Quisp and Quake can sell for as much as $800. The 1970 Nabisco Wheat Honeys or Rice Honeys featuring Beatles stickers and the yellow submarine on the front is the collector's holy grail, bringing as much as $2000."
>
> from *The Breakfast Cereal Gourmet* by David Hoffman

dubbed "cherry-pickers" by marketers and "crazy" by some of our own friends and family.

I reached the point of no return when I discovered there was a whole world of refunding and couponing beyond the Sunday inserts. Like the addict searching for their next fix, I centered my life on the next big deal. I looked for pads of forms everywhere I went, from those posted on the store shelf to on-package coupons and rebates. I loved the free things, the boxes delivered to my front door, the full mailbox and bathroom shelves bowing with the weight of the bottles of shampoo, tubes of toothpaste, cleaners, and health and beauty items that only cost me pennies. As my family grew and I made the decision to stay home with my children, I liked being able to stretch our budget in such a creative way, and got a real sense of satisfaction from shopping the sales with my coupons.

It didn't take long to realize just how different I was than the average shopper, however. As I got more deeply involved in couponing and refunding, my extreme enthusiasm for the hobby was dampened only by the reaction I got from others when I attempted to share the sagas of my good deals. Initially, I was deluded into thinking that the only thing that kept them from doing what I did was their lack of knowledge. So I frequently, and at great lengths, detailed my shopping sprees.

"Guess what I saved with Venture's double coupons today?" I would gush on the phone to a friend, only to be greeted with a dead silence on the other end. Then she might lamely ask what I could possibly do with all the merchandise I'd obtained. What would we do with it? We had six children then. We'd use it eventually, share it, barter with it, or even sell it. After all, free is free.

"Crest toothpaste is on sale for $1, and Sunday's newspaper had $1 coupons in it!" I'd announce, brimming with excitement at the prospect of free toothpaste.

"I already have a tube of toothpaste," came the perplexed reply.

More than once, I began a conversation detailing a recent shopping trip or the latest great deal, only to abruptly stop talking when I saw my companion's eyes glaze over. Gradually it dawned on me that not everyone else was thrilled by free shampoo and toothpaste. In fact, I realized, while my hobby seemed tedious to some, it was downright bizarre to others.

Was I actually that weird, that different from the average consumer? I knew there were other women like me, who were just as crazy about couponing as I was. I traded with some, and saw others in the grocery store aisles with their coupons. I read about them in the refund magazines I subscribed to. But, admittedly, among my family and friends, I was an oddity.

What was it about couponing and refunding that appealed to me, and not to others? What got me started in this incredibly rewarding hobby? Certainly my mother had used a few coupons but never to any great extent. For one thing, she and my father could barely afford the newspapers or magazines that carried the coupons. As parents raising ten children on a low income, they struggled just to put food on the table and clothes on our backs. My father raised chickens for their eggs and meat and planted and tended a huge garden every year. My mother canned or froze their abundant harvest, sewed many of our clothes, made our dolls, braided rag rugs, and gutted the chickens that became a staple of our Sunday dinners.

If using coupons was simply a matter of saving money and the product of a person's upbringing, then one would presume that most of my siblings, also raised in poverty, would be avid couponers as well. While they are frugal and shop thrift stores, of the ten of us, I was the only one that could be described as a coupon enthusiast until one sister joined me in the hobby last year.

Was it something innate in my personality then that attracted me to couponing and refunding? As a child I had the makings of a future coupon queen, volunteering to clip coupons from the inserts my dad brought home from his Sunday morning newspaper route. In the summer of 1969, when I was just ten years old, I spotted an offer for a free Wham-O Super Ball on the back of the Cheerios box and asked my mother if I could send in the box bottoms for it. I saved enough labels to order balls for myself and each of my nine siblings. While they certainly enjoyed the toy, they felt no compulsion to order one themselves. My mother humored my forays into her cabinets seeking more offers and additional labels. Even then, something about getting shiny quarters taped to postcards and crisp dollar bills tucked inside envelopes addressed in my name gave me a certain thrill, a thrill not shared by everyone, not even my frugal mother.

What is the profile of the average coupon user? How about the extreme coupon user, those of us who are crazy about coupons? What motivates one person to become obsessed with the savings that coupons can offer? How many of us are out there? And what effect do we have on the bottom line for retail stores? Once I began researching who uses coupons and why, I began wondering about the history of couponing and refunding itself.

I chose Psychology as my major in college precisely because I'm always wondering why, dissecting every situation, and questioning what makes another person tick. I used this degree, which I earned in 1985, to research the phenomena of coupon use and the socio-cultural and socioeconomic factors that construct it. In this case, not only am I an observer of this fascinating topic, I've also been a participant. In delving into the why behind coupon use, I hoped to unearth the secrets and motivation behind avid deal-seekers and extreme coupon users among consumers. I am not alone in pondering questions such as these. It seems there is an entire science devoted to studying just this type of thing.

The Science of Shopping

My mission one day was a drastically discounted coffeemaker, which I had spotted in the Sunday sales ad. The layout of the store confused me as soon as I set foot in the door. The aisles went in a somewhat circular pattern, racks on either side soon obliterating any sign of either entrance or exit. Disoriented, I ended up in the women's lingerie section where I'd spotted a prominent "70% off" sign. Despite my best intentions, I left the store with two bags of clearance merchandise, along with the coffeemaker I'd come for.

Some store designers deliberately create spaces that will be confusing so that customers become disoriented, losing control of their ability to make good purchasing decisions, which results in impulse buys. This is called "The Gruen Transfer," a psychological phenomenon named after Victor Gruen, an Austrian-born architect who designed one of the earliest shopping malls in America. The classic signs that someone is experiencing the Gruen Transfer are a dropped jaw, slightly glazed eyes, and a hazy, confused feeling. By the time they reach this point, many people will have slowed down their walking pace. Ironically, Gruen himself disliked the level of manipulation necessary to trigger this mental state, and his intention was to create shopping malls that didn't confuse consumers into buying things they didn't need. We all know how that worked out. Even stores that don't employ disarming design tactics still use strategic spatial arrangements in their displays to encourage impulse buying.

As a mother of young children, I rarely shopped at Gap stores, even though I truly love their soft cotton outfits and girl's decorated socks and underpants. Except for the slashed clearance prices, their clothes were just too pricey. When I did visit one, I headed straight toward the clearance racks. It didn't matter what mall I frequented, the racks were always located in the same place—in a corner at the back wall. After I'd gathered my sale items and began navigating back towards the checkout counter, I'd inevitably be confronted by signs that were turned to face customers coming from that end of the store. Once I reached the counter, I would be greeted with yet more signage offering additional savings if I signed up for their store credit card, and occasionally, a bin or display of a lower-priced items that hadn't been moving off the shelves fast enough.

None of this is done by accident. It is all part of a marketing strategy devised by someone who has studied consumer behavior.

Strategic placement of sale racks and signs is all part of the store's marketing plan, which is designed specifically to entice the shopper to purchase more. The sale-priced merchandise is located in the back so price-conscious consumers, like me, have to navigate the entire store to get to it and the signs are turned so they catch the eye on the way back to the checkout. From the time a consumer sets foot in a store until the second they leave, forces of behavioral psychology and marketing ploys are at work, increasing the odds that shoppers will stay longer and buy more. Even lighting and sound cues are taken into account, playing into all of our senses.

Grocery stores have long employed these kinds of tactics to increase sales. From the pleasant smell of fresh-baked bread wafting through the store, to the highest priced merchandise placed at eye-level, someone, somewhere, came up with specific marketing plans in response to the study of consumer behavior, also known as market research.

Stores use visual cues like bargain bins, hanging promotional signs and endcap displays. Or, they may compare a sale price to a list price, except that the list price has been hiked up to reflect a deeper discount. The savvy consumer might have a rudimentary understanding of the concept of loss-leaders and how companies pay to have their product featured on an endcap, but be totally unaware of the more subtle ways businesses influence public buying behavior. In fact, stores count on the majority of consumers to be blissfully ignorant of their marketing strategies.

In preparation for writing this book, I took a crash course in consumer behavior and marketing by reading books like *Consumer Behavior for Dummies* and *Why We Buy*, along with delving into research related to consumer behavior and shopping. While Procter & Gamble had created a research department as far back as 1923, consumer behavior remained a relatively new field of study in the mid-1960s. It has now become one of the main topics in contemporary marketing education at universities and colleges, with several books focusing on the topic as well as magazines like *The Journal of Consumer Psychology* which include a dozen new research studies in each issue.

In layman's terms, the study of consumer behavior means getting into the head of the consumer to figure out the motives behind their purchases. We've all heard someone say something along the lines of, "I *need* that purse," or "those shoes," or "that wide-screen television," things they most definitely do not actually *need*. What we do *need* is food, water, and shelter. There are certainly plenty of marketing techniques employed to get us to buy a particular product, especially in regards to the first item in that category: food.

Companies have ample opportunities to promote their products. Where is the milk located in the grocery store where you shop? Everyone needs milk, but if that is all we plan to buy, we are forced to go through the entire store to get to the dairy case in the back. Need to pick up a prescription at the local drugstore? The pharmacy is also located at the back of the store, ensuring you must pass several shelves of strategically placed merchandise and sale racks of gifts you didn't even know you wanted, but suddenly appeal to you. When you reach the checkout, displays of candy, gum, breath mints, eyeglass repair kits, batteries, and pain relief medication entice the consumer to purchase just one more thing.

None of this is left to coincidence. When a business understands consumer behavior, they can design marketing plans to influence purchasing decisions. Consumers are at least marginally aware of this. They were wary of advertising as long ago as 1925, when crusading journalist Stuart Chase took direct aim at commercial advertising in his book *Tragedy of Waste* and two years later, at corporate manufacturers in *Your Money's Worth: A Study in the Waste of the Consumer's Dollars*. But it was Vance Packard's 1957 *The Hidden Persuaders* that really blew the lid off of corporate advertising and motivational research. According to the *Wiley International Encyclopedia of Marketing* (2010), questions such as "Why are ice cream containers round?" or "Where did the maternal Betty Crocker appearance come from?" are related to a form of consumer research called "motivation research," a term used to refer to research methods designed to probe consumer's minds to discover the deep, often subconscious reasons and goals underlying everyday consumer behaviors. Motivation research was the premier consumer research method used in the 1950s.

Sigmund Freud's psychoanalytic theories on deeply hidden needs and drives underlying all human behavior provided the foundation for the development of motivation research in marketing. Ernest Dichter, often referred to as the "father of motivational research," was a trained psychoanalyst in Vienna who moved to New York in 1938. The founder of The Institute for Motivational Research,

"A man in love is like a clipped coupon—it's time to cash in."

—Mae West

he began applying psychoanalytical techniques to the study of consumer buying habits, using qualitative research methods to delve deep into the consumer psyche. A *New York Times* article in 1998 stated that he was the first to coin the term "focus group" and to stress the importance of image and persuasion in advertising.

According to Vance Packard, market research, or MR as he calls it in *The Hidden Persuaders*, took root as a serious movement in the late forties and early fifties. One of the first milestones of market research in printed form appeared in the April 1950 issue of the *Journal of Marketing* published by the American Marketing Association. That landmark issue contained four major articles dealing with the depth approach of market research. Within a few months, *Printer's Ink*, a merchandising journal, would run an article by James Vicary explaining how psychiatric methods could be applied to market research.

In an updated, and slightly twisted version of Packard's book, *The Ubiquitous Persuaders*, author George Parker points out that despite Packard's stressing Dichter's influence, Louis Cheskin may have had even more influence on modern methods of motivational research. In the early 1930s, Cheskin embarked on what would become a lifelong obsession to understand how customers' perceptions motivated their behavior. He pioneered the process of eye tracking to determine how people read packaging and advertising. While Dichter relied primarily on Freudian psychology to explain buying behavior, Cheskin's work was based more on logic. For example, while both men worked in cigarette advertising, Dichter claimed that women smoked more when ads depicted "erect" cigarettes in the hands and mouths of other women because of their "penis envy," while Cheskin concluded that women smoked more when they saw other women smoking—a sort of peer influence. Parker reminds the reader of his book that while Cheskin is remembered for many successes, including the Marlboro Man and the Gerber baby, Dichter was widely recognized for telling the management of Mattel to make Barbie's chest bigger, reflecting his Freudian background.

According to James P. Othmer's book *AdLand*, one of the earliest advertising executives to use motivational research in designing advertisements was Leo Burnett. Burnett started his own agency in 1935. His first client was the Minnesota Valley Canning Company with the Jolly Green Giant campaign. When it came to television ads, however, the Jolly Green Giant didn't work so well. The company settled on using him as a giant standing in a valley, giving his trademark laugh. In 1968, Leo Burnett came up with a new campaign, one with a little green sprout who ran around the valley getting into all sorts of trouble and charming the television viewers. Burnett went on to create some of the most memorable brand characters in advertising history, including Morris the Cat, Charlie Tuna, Tony the Tiger, and the Pillsbury Doughboy. He was at the forefront of a group of admen who took market research beyond statistics and applied it on a subconscious level. Othmer quotes him as saying, "Good advertising doesn't just circulate information. It penetrates the public mind with desires and beliefs."

"The consumer isn't a moron; she is your wife."

David Ogilvy,
Confessions of an Advertising Man

Motivational research hasn't disappeared, though it might now be categorized under market research. Market research has become the key to getting a handle on how consumers behave. In a highly competitive world, companies can't afford to take chances on ideas without looking at what customers want and how they behave in attaining it. Increasingly, they are realizing that the best way to gain understanding of the relationship between people and products is through direct observation of the consumer. Once a radical-sounding, somewhat controversial phenomenon, market research is now accepted as the norm among marketers. Today, most companies and ad agencies employ psychologists or an anthropologist trained in ethnology—the science that breaks down humans into categories like race, culture, sex, and income level, as a part of their mainstream market research.

If you've ever noticed someone observing you in a store (and if they're good at their job, you *won't* even be aware of them) it may not be a secret admirer or the store security making sure you don't pocket that piece of jewelry you've been admiring. Instead, it might actually be someone who is being paid to study you and your shopping behavior. There are field researchers all over the United States who work in the science of shopping, tracking shoppers, and noting everything they do.

Author and consumer analyst Paco Underhill runs just such a company. Envirosell employs a team of trackers that travel the globe, studying consumers so that they can advise companies and businesses how best to market to them. Where is the best place to set a sales rack or a bench for men waiting for their female companions to try clothes on? Where in the store should shopping baskets be placed? Underhill and his patriots gather the pertinent information and unearth the secrets of all sorts of typical consumer behavior that can help a store owner figure out solutions to problems they didn't even know they had.

While research has traditionally included surveys, focus groups, retail sales analysis, and the actual observation of shoppers, like everything else in today's world, it has gone high-tech. Since the 1990s, companies such as Procter & Gamble, Intel Corp, and ConAgra Foods have been experimenting with various methods of computer simulation in studying consumer behavior.

In 2007, Kimberly-Clark's "virtual shopping" in a mobile testing unit in a high-tech studio attracted the attention of *The Wall Street Journal*. The studio allows researchers and designers to get a fast read on new product designs and ad displays without having to stage real-life tests. Instead, testing is done with virtual reality tools. The room, with floor-to-ceiling screens and virtual shopping aisles, recreates in vivid detail the interiors of big retailers. While a major newspaper detailed this high-tech studio, Kimberly-Clark wasn't the first to use a virtual shopping experience.

For more than ten years, big name brands have been turning to companies like VideoMining. Based in State College, Pennsylvania, VideoMining is the leading provider of in-store intelligence for retailers and consumer product manufacturers. They have helped clients such as Kraft, Kellogg's, Hershey Foods, Nestlé, and Clorox optimize their shopper marketing and merchandising.

Going one step further, General Mills, with their "Corner Market" in Minnesota and the Frito-Lay SMART Learning Center in Dallas, have built entire centers just for consumer behavior studies. Using the faux supermarket allows researchers to study shopping behavior in a familiar environment, that of an actual store. The store "lab" uses multiple methodologies to study the shopper's behaviors, including transaction tracking, survey research, cart tracking, manual observation, and an automated observation that includes "heat maps" that show where shoppers are spending the most time amongst the displays.

By 2010, two Food Lion lab stores were using 120 overlapping cameras to track and analyze consumers' transactions from the point of entry until their purchases. In addition to the cameras, VideoMining Corporation uses a sophisticated type of facial recognition software that can tell them exactly what age group is buying a product and what kind of display is catching their eye. Of course, shoppers in both stores are informed that cameras are observing their every move, making a skeptic like me wonder if, in fact, the shopper's movements and shopping decisions are genuine and actually reflect their normal shopping behavior.

No longer is it enough to observe consumers in the store or while they are shopping. In order to tailor their products to the consumer, companies will even follow their subject home. For their Old Spice line, Procter & Gamble videotaped men (in swim-

suits) taking showers, leading to the discovery that many men used their body wash for their hair, which resulted in the creation of a line of combination body wash/shampoo. Kimberly-Clark placed special goggles with tiny cameras on consumers

PROCTER & GAMBLE BOX 217, NEVADA, IOWA

They're FREE!

YOU SAVE MONEY!

"Advertising is the rattling of a stick inside a swill bucket."
George Orwell, author

LOOK INSIDE

PRINTED IN U.S.A. RETURN POSTAGE GUARANTEED

to videotape how they bathed and diapered their children, and Arm & Hammer has entered homes to inspect the insides of refrigerators and the conditions of cat litter boxes. The subjects of the research being done at home are often eager to participate, both for the pay and for the chance to be influential in future product designs. Videotaped results of the research are studied and analyzed by product and package designers and marketing executives.

What do these executives do with all the information they gather in the faux supermarkets, focus studies, and observational research? Understanding the consumer is crucial to a product's success. In order to create promotional strategies that speak directly to the potential buyer, marketers first have to understand the "why" behind their decision to purchase.

"Two-thirds of the entire economy is impulse buying," Paco Underhill claimed in his book, *Why We Buy: The Science of Shopping*. Underhill's book was a groundbreaking tome of consumer behavior in 1999, but recent research concurs with his observation. In January of 2010, Market Force (a provider of customer intelligence solutions) conducted a survey of 6,000 consumers to collect data on spending habits and store loyalty, focusing on retail grocery stores and consumer packaged goods.

Market Force was interested in possible patterns of behavior that prompted consumers to try a new product. They focused on six different categories: Cereals, Coffee and Tea, Cleaning Products, Health and Beauty, Snacks, and Beverages. Across all categories, seeing something on the shelf or on an endcap display was responsible for the most trial purchases. Promotions and coupons drove the most new sales for cereals. Within every category, however, retailers could count on one thing: the impulse buy. Even with a grocery list in hand, about a third of respondents would add to their cart a new product that looked interesting, 40 percent would add an indulgence to their cart, and a whopping 89 percent would add a sale item that looks like a bargain.

The key word, in case you missed it, is *looks*. Consumers across the board love a good deal. But sometimes, what looks like a good deal, really isn't one. How is the average shopper supposed to know the difference? That was what concerned Vance Packard in the 1950s and continues to plague the modern consumer today.

Sometimes maturity and experience is the best teacher of all. As a mother of young children in the 1980s, one of my favorite sales gimmicks was the "blue light special" at our local Kmart. It was created in the 1960s as a way for store managers to draw shoppers' attention to slow-moving merchandise that was sold at a special discount for a very limited time. There was usually a ten-minute time frame in which the customer had to select their purchases and get them relabeled with the discount before the light was moved to a different section of the store.

I'd be shopping with our two young children when I'd see the blue light flashing. I can vividly remember how I felt as I rushed to the area of the store where the light flashed—the heady rush of adrenaline, the sweaty palms, and quickened heartbeat. It was an effective promotional tool, as I almost always found some-thing when I frantically perused the sale rack or shelf. It was only later, at home, I might pull my purchases out of the shopping bag, perplexed as to what had possessed me to buy four shirts that didn't yet fit either of my children, and when I looked more closely, weren't even a style I cared for. I almost always experienced buyer's remorse after my trips to Kmart. I was the hapless victim of a popular combination of sales tactic maneuvers, the urgency of the limited-time deal, and the illusion of a slashed discounted price. I eventually stopped chasing the blue light, but I never stopped looking for clearance signs. I would succumb to many sales tactics in the ensuing years, but falling for the blue light special was a rookie mistake—the "good deal" that really wasn't.

One of my daughters coined the phrase "It made me read it," about the pull of a good book, and I intimately understand the concept. For any avid reader, there exists that phenomenon of being unable to stop reading until we've turned that last page. For me, it is any book by author Jodi Picoult. Never mind my best intentions, I've learned from experience to never begin one of her books unless I am certain I'll have the time to finish it by day's end. The bleary-eyed daughter unable to be roused in the morning because of binge reading in the bathroom or underneath her covers until four in the morning said it best, "That book made me read it."

So it is with the heavily discounted merchandise and the clearance items I had coupons for. "I had to buy it," I'd explain to my perplexed husband. "It was 90% off and free with my coupons." That is why a coupon enthusiast might come home with bags of cat treats when they don't have any pets or ten packages of Lunchables with fruit when their children don't even like the product. For most of my life, I just couldn't resist a sale price, especially when a coupon resulted in a free item, or something that cost just pennies with the extra savings.

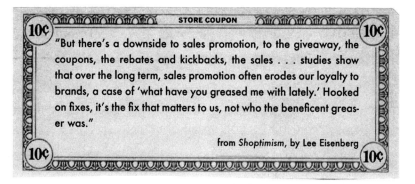

STORE COUPON

"But there's a downside to sales promotion, to the giveaway, the coupons, the rebates and kickbacks, the sales . . . studies show that over the long term, sales promotion often erodes our loyalty to brands, a case of 'what have you greased me with lately.' Hooked on fixes, it's the fix that matters to us, not who the beneficent greaser was."

from *Shoptimism*, by Lee Eisenberg

Coupons are just one of the many ways manufacturers entice the consumer to purchase their product. But what makes one person respond so strongly to a coupon or rebate offer while another ignores the sale price or the coupons entirely? These are the types of questions companies ask all the time.

The bottom line with all the time and money spent on shopper research and consumer studies is that companies want to know what people are buying and why. More importantly, they want to know how to get the consumer to buy more. There's a method to the madness of volume discounts ("Buy 10 for $10"), and the secret lies in the perception of the shopper. Bargain appeals have been proven to work in getting the consumer to purchase more than they normally would because they perceive the price as a good deal, even when it isn't. The consumer reading this should remember: A bargain isn't always a bargain, and a "good deal" might just be a marketer's way of taking advantage of your perception as to what constitutes a deal. Remember my intention to purchase a coffeemaker and the subsequent detour to a "70% off" rack? Those two bags of clearance merchandise I left the store with were overpriced in the first place. It turns out that the "70% off" clearance price was comparable to the discount store's regular price on similar merchandise. Did I really get a good deal, or had I fallen for yet another sales ploy?

Information gathered from consumer research is used to design these kinds of marketing tactics, along with media relations campaigns. And whether that is television and newspaper ads or targeting the consumer with some form of promotion, the purpose is the same. The contest, giveaway, rebate, and yes, the mighty coupon is utilized for one reason: to sell more stuff.

And companies have been using the coupon aspect of promotions for a very long time. For over one hundred years, in fact.

3¢

Coupon
Chronicles

For thirty-two years I went shopping with my coupon box in tow without ever seeing another consumer with either a coupon box or binder. Not once. I spotted small coupon wallets that fit in a purse or envelopes of coupons, but never a box or binder. By early 2011, I was beginning to see women with coupon binders everywhere I went. All of a sudden, couponing was hot. It was as if couponing was a totally new concept, and yet coupons had been around for over 125 years.

The coupon as a form of marketing and promotion was introduced in the late 1880s, when a voucher for a free glass of Coca-Cola was distributed under the ownership of John Pemberton, who invented the product in 1886. Pemberton gradually sold portions of his business to partners, and then Asa G. Candler, a brilliant Atlanta businessman, achieved sole ownership of the company in 1891. Candler expanded on the innovative idea of giving out a complimentary Coca-Cola. His handwritten coupons offered a free glass of the beverage that was selling only nine glasses a day in its first year. Distributed on the streets of Atlanta, then through the mail and company salesmen, by 1913 an estimated 8.5 million free drink coupons had been redeemed. It seems a daring move—a company giving away its product— but it proved to be an effective one.

Coupled with an aggressive campaign to get Coca-Cola's name plastered on everything from calendars to apothecary scales, coupons were at least partially responsible for Coca-Cola becoming a household name. For someone with such remarkable business sense, Candler proved to lack the foresight to imagine a future demand for a portable beverage. In 1899, he sold exclusive rights to bottle the drink for the grand sum of one dollar. Despite the success of the Coca-Cola campaign, the idea of using coupons as a promotional tool didn't immediately catch on. It wasn't until 1897 that C. W. Post issued a one-cent coupon to introduce his new breakfast cereal, Grape Nuts. Other cereal companies soon followed suit. Coupon use increased during the Depression when it was essential for families to find ways to stretch their budgets. Chain supermarkets began offering them in the 1940s as a way to draw customers away from neighborhood markets.

After the Depression, consumers kept up their habit of saving money through coupon clipping, and an entire industry developed. By 1957, there was a clearing house devoted solely

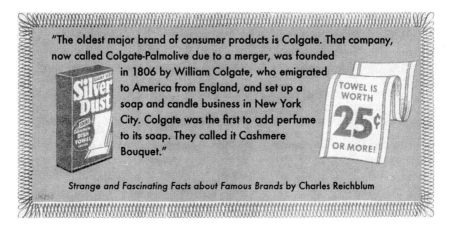

"The oldest major brand of consumer products is Colgate. That company, now called Colgate-Palmolive due to a merger, was founded in 1806 by William Colgate, who emigrated to America from England, and set up a soap and candle business in New York City. Colgate was the first to add perfume to its soap. They called it Cashmere Bouquet."

Strange and Fascinating Facts about Famous Brands by Charles Reichblum

to the redemption of coupons. Initially called the Nielson Coupon Clearing House, the name was eventually changed to the Manufacturers Coupon Control Center, or MC3.

By 1965, more than half of the people in the United States reported using coupons. Ten years later, that number grew to 75 percent. By the end of the twentieth century, using coupons had become a part of shopping for the majority of families. According to Inmar, a network of independent marketing consultants, the peak year for coupon redemption was 1992, at the end of the last recession, when 7.9 billion coupons were redeemed. This period was followed by a fifteen-year decline in use. Still, coupons had become a natural way of life for most families. So much so that in 1998 the United States designated September as "National Coupon Month," despite the fact that in 2007, less than 3 percent of all manufacturers' coupons distributed via newspapers, magazines, or in the mail were actually redeemed.

Slumps in the economy do seem to contribute to resurgence in their use. According to Inmar, an increase in redemption was noted in October 2008, when the US financial crisis hit. Over three billion coupons were redeemed in 2009, a 27 percent leap from the 2.6 billion redeemed in 2008. Marketers responded in kind, by increasing the number of coupons distributed to the public. CouponInfoNow, sponsored by Inmar, reported that major brands issued 367 billion coupons in 2009, at an average face value of $1.44, an investment that indicated their commitment to promotions. The rise in coupon distribution and redemption continued into 2010, with an end-of-the-year report by NCH Marketing Services reporting that shoppers saved 3.7 billion dollars with coupons in 2010, a 5.7 percent increase from 2009. Marketers distributed 332 billion consumer packaged goods (CPG) coupons in 2010, the largest single-year distribution quantity ever recorded in the United States. Following those two record-breaking years coupon distribution in the CPR market stabilized in the first half of 2011. In a July 2011 mid-year report, NCH Marketing Services reported that consumers saved 2 billion dollars with coupons just in the first half of the year. According to NCH, a Valassis Company, by the third quarter of 2012, Consumer Package Goods (CPG) market-ers were offering fewer and less attractive coupons to consumers, bringing the previous three years of coupon redemption growth to an abrupt halt. There was considerable variability across brands, companies, and categories, however, which diverged from the overall market trend. While there were 3.5 percent fewer grocery coupons being issued, there was actually a 10.4 percent increase in the amount of health and beauty coupons being issued. Those brands offering fewer coupons may have unintentionally given a competitive advantage to those who were still offering generous, high value coupons, as well as to store brands.

Overall, CPG marketers distributed 165 billion coupons during the first half of 2012, but grocery manufacturers cut distribution by a full 7 percent. Savvy consumers, who were used to saving money on groceries with coupons, noticed the difference, too. While coupon redemption rose 34.7 percent from 2008 to 2011, third quarter statistics in 2012 showed a 17 percent decrease in redemption rate. No wonder; we were still able to save on our razors and shampoo, but just as prices on groceries were rising, fewer food coupons were being offered. With fewer coupons and a lower average face value of those offered, using coupons apparently became less appealing.

Where does the modern consumer find most of their coupons? Well, some things never change. Like the first Coca-Cola and Post cereal coupons, the majority, nearly 90 percent, are still found in the Sunday newspaper. Then there are the coupons found in store ads, on the packages, inside magazines, in direct mail and store handouts, and of course, the electronic and digital coupons. All of these categories have experienced growth since 2005, but none at the level of Internet-printed and mobile coupons. With the proliferation of the Internet, the face of couponing has naturally morphed somewhat. The Internet has opened up a whole new world for customer savings (and for fraud, but more on that later). IndustryStatistics.com reported in an April 2011 internet retailer report that 74 percent of consumers search multiple online coupon resources each week, identifying four major types of online coupons:

- **Internet-Printed coupons**: Internet-printed (IP) coupons are one of the fastest emerging developments in the world of savings. Internet printed coupons are just what they sound like: coupons that can be downloaded and printed out to take to the store.

- **Store loyalty cards**: Advances in technology have prompted grocery stores to offer more innovative ways for their customers to save money. Some offer club membership discounts or store savings cards, which also allows the store a handy way of tracking consumer purchases. Other stores offer a savings that can be loaded onto a card from the customer's home computer.

- **Mobile coupons**: One of the fastest growing types of coupons used today is the mobile coupon, or a coupon that is offered via a text message. The new coupon-savvy consumer doesn't even have to use a scissors for their savings.

- **Online shopping discount codes**: The coupon codes are a combination of numbers and/or letters that can be entered into a promotional code section on an online order form, offering a savings that is deducted from the total purchase at checkout.

There are those in the industry who argue that paper coupons are a thing of the past, despite evidence to the contrary. Coupons have been around since the nineteenth century and are a part of most consumers' lives. Obviously, from current trends and in tough economic times, the mighty coupon has become a means of saving money, even for those who don't normally clip them.

What happens if manufacturers don't respond to the consumer demand for more coupons, or worse, withhold what has been one of the consumer's favorite promotions? Is couponing still an effective promotional strategy?

Let's look to Proctor & Gamble to answer that question. In January of 2001, the *Journal of Marketing* published a study on the effects of Procter & Gamble's decision to reduce its coupon distribution from 1990 to 1996. The study looked across 24 categories at the effects of the company's 20.7 percent increase in advertising, 15.7 percent decrease in trade deals, and 54.3 percent decrease in coupons. Proctor & Gamble's net prices also rose 20.4 percent during this same seven-year period.

What were the results of this experiment? Proctor & Gamble lost roughly 18 percent in marketing share. The study concluded that promotion (rather than advertising) has a stronger impact on market share for the average Consumer Packaged Goods (CPG) and that decreasing coupon promotions decreases market share-without any effect on brand loyalty. In fact, coupon loyalty could be more important than brand loyalty. Toward the end of the study's research period, Proctor & Gamble conducted a well-publicized "zero coupon test" in Upstate New York. Proctor & Gamble discontinued distributing coupons in this area and replaced them with lower prices. The result was a public relations nightmare where consumers boycotted, held public hearings, and petitioned local politicians to take action. The ensuing anti-trust litigation resulted in a $4.2 million settlement. Tellingly, Proctor & Gamble paid out their portion of the settlement in the form of $2 coupons.

Cold cereal manufacturers tried a similar tactic with dismal results. According to a 2000 *Food Review* article, coupons have consistently been the predominant promotional strategy used by the Ready To Eat (RTE) cereal industry. In 1993, the redemption rate for RTE cereal coupons was 3.8 percent as compared with 2.2 percent for all grocery coupons. In April 1996, Post slashed prices on its entire product line by 20 percent so it could reduce its reliance on couponing. They also lowered the face value of the coupons they did distribute. Within months, two other big-name cereal manufacturers followed suit, with General Mills cutting the prices of nearly half their cereals by 11 percent and Kellogg's dropping the prices of their brands that competed directly with Post cereals by 19 percent. The industry's profitability dropped and sales remained static.

"The average person consumes about ten pounds, or 160 bowls of cereal per year."

The Breakfast Cereal Gourmet
by David Hoffman

My personal reaction to the decline in cereal coupons was to resort to muffins and toast. With ready-to-eat cereals especially, coupon use remains extremely important to the consumer. CouponInfoNow reports that 75 percent of consumers say they usually use coupons to purchase breakfast cereal.

It isn't just the food and health and beauty coupons that consumers are attached to either. When Macy's department store chain cut back on their coupons in May of 2007, their customer visits dropped dramatically and Macy's had to acknowledge that their customers had been turned off by the move. Within a year, they'd reinstated coupons.

"They reduced the coupons, which everybody loves, and it was a disaster," said Howard Davidowitz, chairman of Davidowitz & Associates, a New York-based retail consulting firm, in a *Baltimore Sun* article. "You have tens of millions of people who their whole driver of shopping is coupons. It's not just something you can take away."

Some companies have to learn their lesson the hard way. Take J. C. Penney, for instance. According to *Bloomberg Businessweek*, former Apple Store Chief Ron Johnson planned to wean J. C. Penney's customers from their diet of coupons when he took over as CEO in 2011. Instead, he immediately discontinued coupons and replaced J. C. Penney's high prices with lower, everyday prices, their "Fair and Square" pricing plan. The department store chain lost 163 million dollars in the first three months of his plan, and the number of people coming into J. C. Penney's dropped by 10 percent.

"What is the source of this?" asked Mike Kramer, J. C. Penney's Chief operating officer in 2012. "Coupons, that drug. We did not realize how deep some of the customers were into this. We have got to wean them off this and educate our customers."

"I thought people were just tired of coupons," J. C. Penney's CEO Ron Johnson said in a *Businessweek* interview. "The reality is, there were a certain part of the customers that loved it. I didn't understand that."

Despite the company's revenue dropping 20 percent in the first quarter after introducing the "Fair and Square Pricing Plan," Johnson vowed that their stores wouldn't be reinstating coupons anytime soon. There was hope and hype among avid couponers when a "$10 off" coupon was issued to e-mail subscribers in October of 2012, which Johnson insisted on calling a "gift." By the end of 2012, the department store retailer had lost 4.3 billion dollars of sales from the previous year, nearly one-third of its sales, according to a February 2013 Financial Times report.

"It's the worst performance I have ever seen by a company in one year," Walter Loeb, a veteran retail consultant said in Yahoo Business and Finance report.

With dismal reports like this, Johnson was ready to acknowledge the error of his ways by the end of February 2013. "Experience is making mistakes and learning from them, and I have learned a lot," Johnson was quoted as saying in the Yahoo Business and Finance report. "We learned she (the customer) prefers a sale. At times, she loves a coupon."

Johnson's reluctant admission regarding the value of sales and coupons was evidently too little, too late. He was ousted as CEO in April of 2013.

The damning results of their one year experiment eliminating coupons was similar to those of Stein Mart, Inc. Stein Mart stores reduced their available coupons by 20 percent in 2011, in a move towards lower everyday pricing. "It got so out of hand that we had to reign it back in," Jay Stein, interim president and CEO remarked in *Orlando Business Journal*. "We don't want our customers to think they have to use a coupon to get a better price at Stein Mart."

Stein Mart simplified their pricing, reducing coupons by 50 percent in 2012 to get away from the falsely high price tags, similar to the J. C. Penney's lower pricing strategy. The impact was dramatic. Total sales initially fell 2.2 percent for the fourth quarter in 2011. Yet by September 2012 sales reports show an increased 2 percent. Perhaps the difference was that Stein Mart *decreased* coupons, but did not eliminate them entirely.

Bed Bath & Beyond stores seem well aware of which side of their bread is buttered. While their CEO is continually blaming declines in their profits on an increase in their available coupons, he has stubbornly refused to do away with the promotional "20% off" coupons. Why? Perhaps because they don't want to lose their core of coupon-happy shoppers, the same core of coupon clippers who evidently stopped shopping at J. C. Penney stores when they discontinued their coupons.

"Like it or not, consumers are addicted to coupons, and they count on them," Susan M. Jones, vice president of business development and marketing at CMS, Inc., which tracks coupon usage, reiterates in a *Baltimore Sun* article.

Yes, consumers can be addicted to using coupons. I freely admit my own addiction. Not only that, but as an avid refunder in the 1980s and 1990s, I was equally addicted to getting free things.

For those of us who have been in the coupon buisiness for any length of time, refunding used to be synonymous with couponing. According to David Vaczek and Richard Sale in an August 1998 *Promo* magazine article about advertising promotions, refunds and premium offers also have a long history as a promotional tactic, going back as far as the early 1880s when Adolphus Busch, a beer seller from St. Louis, used to park his beer wagon in front of a saloon to give out free samples and premiums like jack-knives, stick pins, and watch fobs to his favorite customers. Refunds, unlike their coupon counterparts, offer a certain amount of money or a premium, like a T-shirt, hat, or stuffed toy sent to the buyer of the product in exchange for the consumer sending in certain proofs of purchase to the company. One hundred years after Busch's knife giveaway, the vast amount of premium refund offers available would boggle the mind of any 1880s salesman. By the 1980s, it was easy for me to stock a Christmas gift cupboard with free crayons, balls, hats, T-shirts, towels, and stuffed animals, not to mention all the cash-back offers that could easily add up to almost 100 dollars a month.

A typical refund back then might simply request four UPCs or ten wrappers, of which the avid refunder would already have in their files, waiting for just such an offer. Before the advent of UPC codes, manufacturers might ask for a net weight statement for one offer and a boxtop for another, so the savvy refunder saved the entire package from the products they bought. Cash register tapes were rarely needed, except for some of the more lucrative offers like money back on a liquor purchase or car tires. Manufacturers counted on a certain amount of "slippage" with these offers, using the special offer to motivate the customer to purchase the product, knowing that a good percentage of consumers would inevitably forget to send for the refund. Hardcore refunders, however, didn't let anything slip by them. If it was free, they sent for it, even if it was a cat toy and they had no pets.

Mail-in rebates, or instant rebates, are still used as a promotional tool, especially for electronics and other big-ticket items. They're offered either by the retailer or the manufacturer. Now, many of the forms are printed right at the cash register at the time of purchase, or just like in the

"When credit cards first appeared in the early 1950s, they were made of paper. Plastic cards weren't produced until 1959."

Strange and Fascinating Facts About Famous Brands by Charles Reichblum

good old days, a separate form is required to mail in for the refund. Most offers are handled under contract by a clearinghouse that specializes in processing rebates and contest entries.

With fewer premium and cash back refunds today, it is no longer a given that an avid coupon user will also be a refunder, or that those of us who did refunds, still do. Most of us had abandoned saving and neatly filing our trash years ago. The new generation isn't even familiar with the term "refund," instead using the word "rebate." Still, for the extreme coupon user, the idea of getting their money back on products they purchase is appealing, a good deal made even better with the added incentive to purchase.

Marketers take note, it appears as though coupons are here to stay and that they appeal to a large segment of the consumer population. The average consumer uses them to some degree, saving anywhere from five to ten dollars a week on their grocery bill. But, then, this book is not about the average coupon user. It is about the consumers who are saving much more than ten dollars a week on their groceries.

Who Are the Coupon Crazy?

You've likely seen one on television or in the newspaper—the self-proclaimed "Coupon Queen" who buys 100 dollars' worth of groceries for less than 10 dollars. A March 2010 *Nightline* exclusive featured a shopping duel between two of them: Nathan Engels, a male couponer nicknamed "Mr. Coupon," who greeted the news crew with the tower he constructed with free boxes of Jell-O, and Jill Cataldo, a "Coupon Queen" who teaches couponing classes in Chicago and writes a nationally syndicated column. Television station TLC built an entire series, *Extreme Couponing*, around the most extreme, and sometimes controversial, of America's coupon users. Maybe you grew up in a house where your mother dutifully clipped every coupon. Perhaps your friend or sister is an avid coupon user. Or maybe, like me, you count yourself among them.

The shopping trips planned for the media are generally set up for spectacular results that might not be typical even for that particular shopper, although depending upon store doubling opportunities, they can be. In regards to the *Extreme Couponing* program, cases of certain products have been ordered ahead of time and shelves stocked in proportions that aren't readily available to the general public. In other words, the average shopper is physically unable to perform the fantastic shopping feats shown on this reality-based program that, in fact, doesn't resemble reality in the least.

I was approached by the *Extreme Couponing* team for the possibility of inclusion in their program on three separate occasions, and each time I reiterated that it was nearly impossible in Iowa to replicate the type of sprees they featured on their program. I got a peek into the "reality" of the program when I was asked this revealing question: "If we took you to a store that doubled coupons, or found a store that would allow it for the purpose of the program, would you be able to do it?" It was apparent that for an Iowan with no double coupon opportunities, producers of the program would

STORE COUPON

M-111

From Coupons.com list of Frugalebrities of 2011 (celebrities known for savvy shopping habits):

- Sarah Michelle Gellar
- Halle Berry
- Hilary Swank
- Kourtney Kardashian
- Renee Zellweger
- Tim Hasselbeck

M-111

STORE COUPON

have had to transport me out of state for filming, and traveling out of state to shop is hardly a reality for the average Iowan.

I've done the planned media shopping trips—saving free product coupons or arranging a shopping spree specifically around products that will cost just pennies after my coupons. I've seen the reporter and photographer share amused glances at my running commentary as we peruse store aisles together and their confusion over the items I'm choosing to put in my cart. Why would a frugal mother buy ten packages of paper plates? Wouldn't it make more financial sense to use regular plates and wash them? What about those rolls of paper towels? Isn't it more prudent to use rags? I relish their wide-eyed look at the low final total after my coupons are deducted and it dawns on them that those products were totally free after coupon savings. The media loves the "wow" factor, and the audience doesn't disappoint with their incredulous reaction to the "Coupon Queen's" fabulous savings.

But I'm not always walking out of stores with carts full of free merchandise. Outside of the set up shopping trip and rare double coupon opportunities, I might only save a meager 10 to 20 percent off my grocery bill and 80 percent on my health and beauty purchases, still well above the average coupon user's savings.

According to research done by the Promotion Marketing Association (PMA) a typical coupon user reports an average of 7 percent savings on their weekly grocery bills. In a September 2008 press release, the PMA reported that consumers who spend just twenty minutes per week clipping and organizing their coupons can save up to one thousand dollars a year on their annual grocery bill. The typical family saves between five and nine dollars per week using coupons. Forty-six percent of consumers spend just ten minutes clipping and organizing and still achieve an average of seven dollars a week in savings.

4632 BN
12796

TAKE THIS COUPON TO YOUR STORE

10¢

Carol Blank of Parsippany, New Jersey, has been an avid coupon user for as long as she has been married, over forty years. Even though their income is a comfortable $60,000+ a year, Carol loves coupons so much she wasn't about to stop using them after her two children left home. She easily slashes 65 percent off her weekly grocery

10¢

bill and stockpiles enough free paper products and non-perishables that she can regularly donate to local charities.

12796

Reporter Brett Arends did the math in a February, 2010 *Wall Street Journal* article, figuring that with an average value of $1.44 per coupon and a minute's effort to clip, the savings is the equivalent of $14.40 per ten minutes, or $86.40 per hour. And unlike money earned at work, the coupon savings is tax free.

It isn't as simple as that; clipping one coupon doesn't automatically mean a savings. The consumer has to remember to take it to the store and redeem it for that product before there is an actual savings. And even then, if they don't actually need the product or a cheaper generic is available, then the coupon really isn't saving them money at all. Still, Arend's low-finance math perspective is not without merit. It is true; the savings can really add up.

Several years ago, I visited with a friend who began lauding the praises of a new brand of canned chili bean product she'd tried and loved. "I have coupons for those you can have!" I exclaimed. "You can get one free with every can you buy."

"No!" her husband protested from across the room. "No coupons!" His booming baritone stopped me in my tracks. Was he kidding? I wasn't sure, so I looked at my friend.

She leaned in closer and whispered apologetically, "He won't let me use coupons. He thinks only poor people use them."

After I got over the initial embarrassment of being categorized as part of the poor population by her husband, I wondered if there was a grain of truth to his statement. While I knew it wasn't only the poor who used coupons, I did approach the writing of this book with a similar misconception—that it might be those who were either raised in a lower income household or struggling to live on a stringent budget that would be most likely to use them.

It turns out we were both wrong. According to the results of a 2009 survey released by the Nielsen Company, it is actually the opposite; the more affluent consumers—those making $70,000 or more annually—use coupons the most frequently. In fact, households with incomes of $100,000 or more were the primary drivers of coupon growth in 2009. Other serious users included those from large households and consumers living in affluent suburban or "comfortable country areas" on the fringes of larger cities. Groups least likely to use them were low-income, one-member households, male-only head of households, African-Americans, Hispanic consumers, and those living in rural or struggling urban areas.

One explanation for this disparity is the trend relating to newspaper readership. According to New York–based Scarborough Research, it is the well-educated and higher income households that buy and read newspapers more than others, and the newspaper remains the key vehicle for delivering coupons. Additionally, promotions are generally targeted in areas with more affluent consumers.

THIS COUPON WORTH 10¢

H.G. of Pennsylvania is a divorced mother of one. She has a PhD and her income is between $100,000 and $120,000 a year. She's been using coupons ever since she was seven years old when she discovered a one-dollar rebate on a one-dollar pack of pens. Saving money was a value she learned early in life, and it has stayed with her even through the years of advancing both her education and her income. She donates a lot of her extra deals to a local food pantry.

Cash value 1/20th of 1 cent   COLGATE-PALMOLIVE-PEET CO., Jersey City 2, N. J.

So, does that mean that coupon users are a smarter bunch of people? For the purpose of categorization, in a word—yes. Or, at least we'd like to think so. According to a May 2010 WSL Strategic Retail bulletin, 58 percent of respondents said they liked using coupons because it makes them feel smart.

"Coupons give the consumer a tangible form of savings," says Matt Wallaert, a behavioral psychologist and the lead scientist at Churnless.com, a digital strategy and production company. "The coupon users can tell themselves that this little piece of paper that they have cut [out] and redeemed entitles them to a discount that others don't have. It gives the consumer a sense of control over their savings. When they get something free because of the coupon, it is even better. One of the things that makes us feel smart is getting something for free. During a recession, frugal is not a bad word. It's a good word. This is something that people are supposed to be doing. They're searching for free more than ever because it's a symbol of financially savviness." Thus, even a wealthy consumer can feel smarter by using coupons.

But it isn't all about the savings or the feeling of beating the system with a good deal. Ambuj Jain, an assistant marketing professor at Southern Methodist University's Edwin L. Cox School of Business, did a five-year study of 550 households in Buffalo, New York, that suggested the psychological benefits of coupon clipping outweighed even the savings incentives. The results suggested that the very act of clipping was part of the fun. The respondents enjoyed the whole process.

But what about those instances when using coupons makes the consumer feel something less enjoyable, like embarrassment or as an annoyance to the cashier?

A recent study published in the *Journal of Retailing* shows an interesting reason why upper-income whites make far more use of coupons than members of minorities of all income levels. One surprising finding of this study, conducted by Anne Brumbaugh of the College of Charleston and Jose Antonio Rosa of the University of Wyoming, was how much the attitude of the cashier can determine the customer's willingness to use coupons.

A clerk's conscious or subconscious cues such as eye rolls, deep sighs, and terse movements in accepting the coupons can discourage all but the most confident from using them. Conversely, a clerk who implies that the customer is shrewd in their savings can inspire the customer to use them more often.

The study also investigated the reason why even the more affluent members of racial minorities don't often use coupons. They found that a consistent level of poor services experienced by high socioeconomic status black and Latino customers reduced their coupon use by decreasing their confidence and increasing their embarrassment over using them. Well-to-do white consumers, on the other hand, incorporated the use of coupons into the image of what a stay-at-home spouse should do. They were confident enough in their affluence not to feel threatened by the attitude of clerks. Those most sensitive to the criticism received at the checkout (and perhaps from the customers behind them in line) are less likely to be willing to use coupons because they view them as a symbol of financial need.

So, in essence, my friend's husband, who forbade coupon use, was not confident enough in his own financial status to allow his wife to use coupons. I, on the other hand, have definitely been encouraged by enthusiastic cashiers and even praise from customers waiting in line behind me. I've even had a man or two express a wish to be married to me, much to my chagrin, and their wife's extreme annoyance.

On the other hand, I have also experienced negative reactions to my coupon use: the eye rolls, exaggerated sighs, and once, a woman behind me in line (to whom I had offered coupons to use on her order), eyed me up and down in derision, and asked "Do I look like I need to use coupons?"

10¢ 10¢ STORE COUPON

Jennifer R. of Oklahoma has been married for fifteen years and is the mother of four children. Their household income is approximately $140,000 a year. She is a cradle couponer, having learned the fine art of coupon clipping from her mother. While their income is comfortable now, she and her husband operate on the assumption that it might not always be that way. They like to save money wherever they can, and Jennifer can readily contribute to the savings at the grocery store with her coupons. She also donates to a local food bank and women's shelter.

10¢ 10¢

But then, I don't use coupons to have praises lauded upon me for my super savings. That's just a nice bonus. I started using coupons to save money. I kept using them because it turned out to be a fun and rewarding way to shop. At some point, the fun turned into an obsession. There is a subtle difference between the casual couponer and the serious couponer, but there is a world of difference between a casual user and those "crazy" couponers like me: the ones bordering on the edge of freakdom.

Inmar's Advantage Update "The 2009 Consumer Study" segmented coupon users into six distinct groups based on their semi-annual buying habits in the first half of 2009. The coupon user groups were as follows: nonusers, super low users, those who used 1–3 coupons in a six-month period, those super heavy users who used 51–103 coupons in a six-month period, and the final category, "Coupon Enthusiasts," those who used 104 or more in a six-month period.

To the average reader, this kind of categorization makes sense. But to a "shoptimizer," there seems to be one important category left unrepresented. For an example of the missing category, check out my typical shopping habits in early 2012:

Day 1: Saturday: Check the upcoming week's ads and Sunday's coupon inserts online at www. RefundCents.com, and take note of any good deals I want to take advantage of. (*30 minutes to 1 hour*)

Day 2: Sunday: After putting on a pot of coffee, pick up the newspaper off the front porch and, with pad of paper and pen handy, immediately pull out the coupon inserts and ads. Scrutinize both and match up any super deals for the week. Begin writing weekly coupon column, pointing out how to combine that week's sales with the Sunday coupons. Plan a strategy for the week's out-of-town shopping trip, if sales warrant it. (*approximately 1 hour*) Additional work on column. (*1 hour*)

Day 4: Monday: Complete my revised and final coupon column and submit to the newspaper. Print out list of good deals from various online websites like www.RefundCents.com. Read other good deal alerts from chat board, jotting down any that sound promising. Clip coupons while watching television. (*Total time spent on coupon-related activities, including column, 2 hours.*)

Day 5: Tuesday: The ad for our local grocery store comes out. Scan it for good deals. Check coupon binder for corresponding coupons (*15 minutes*). Shop that afternoon with coupon binder in tow. Use 10–15 coupons, depending upon sale prices and what I find in the clearance cart. (*1 hour*)

Day 6: Wednesday: Organize coupon binder. Finalize strategy for out-of town trip. Pick up extra coupons from a teen neighbor who saves them for me. (*30 minutes*)

Day 7: Thursday: (Dependent upon day 6 and the deals available that week.) If an out-of-town trip is planned, leave early in the afternoon after the children have completed their schoolwork for the day. Stop at one or two thrift stores, looking for children's clothing, good books, stationery, and pretty baskets for my workshops. Walgreens is usually the next stop, with anywhere from 10–15 coupons redeemed, along with any of the store's register reward coupons that had been triggered at the register by the previous trip's purchase. Ideally, most of the items in my bags are free. Sometimes a Target shopping spree is involved, if the ad was particularly good. A stop at Hy-Vee for fruit and this week's good deals, using another 10–15 coupons. (*4+ hours*)

Day 8: Friday: Rest up in order to begin the process all over again the next day.

Two things that are obvious from this saga are: 1) I can spend an inordinate amount of time clipping, sorting, and filing coupons, planning the best strategy, and shopping, and 2) I could feasibly use the 104 coupons that qualify me as an enthusiast for a six month period *in just two weeks.* I've used as many as 75 coupons in *one trip* during planned shopping trips where doubling coupons was allowed. I know couponers who regularly use over 100 coupons a week, depending upon their family size, where they live, and the stores in the area that double.

MONEY-SAVING COUPON 10¢

Christine, from Long Island, New York, is married and has two children. She and her husband have a combined income of approximately $200,000 a year. Both she and her husband are avid coupon users. Christine regularly saves 75 percent off her weekly grocery bill. Her husband collects coupon inserts and is instrumental in saving money in other areas of their life. Thanks to their frugality, their house is completely paid off and they own both a vacation home and an investment property. They send their children to a private school and summer camps and enjoy three major vacations a year with the money they save.

TO THE DEALER: Our salesman will redeem this coupon in accordance with the agreement made with you, provided you and the customer have complied with the terms of this offer. The customer must pay any sales tax on the CRISCO received.   PROCTER & GAMBLE

PRINTED IN U.S.A.   MW-4-49   1228-TF

What about the "coupon crazy", those who might be using a thousand or more coupons in a six-month period? How are those people categorized? Combining data from the Inmar 2009 Consumer Study with a Nielsen Manufacturer Coupon Sourcing study shows two key findings of interest:

- 75 percent of all respondents stated that coupons had at least some influence on their decision to purchase a new product.

- 81 percent of all units purchased with a coupon in the first six months of 2009 were bought by 19 percent of all households. (Nielson)

That last statistic bears repeating: 19 percent of all households purchased 81 percent of the items that were bought with coupons. In July 2011, *Advertising Age* published an article which reported a dramatic change in the second half of 2010, according to Nielsen panel data: "Coupon enthusiasts" increased from 11 percent of coupon users in 2009 to 13 percent, and that segment of society was responsible for 70 percent of the coupon purchases in 2010. Is this the missing category, or are the true "coupon crazy" an even smaller percentage of households? Nieslen categorizes "coupon enthusiasts" as those using 104 coupons in a six-month period. What if they broke that down even more? What percentage of those couponers used more than 104 coupons *per month*? From the loaded carts and the stacks of coupons used by participants in the *Extreme Couponing* television show, one could conclude that at least those people are buying 90 percent of their purchases with a coupon.

Could these "extreme" couponers be among the "cherry pickers"—that group most feared by the supermarket industry? Extreme cherry pickers shop only discounted sale items and nothing else, reducing the profit margins. That sounds a lot like me, at least in regards to the health and beauty categories of shopping. Until 2010, when prices went up and coupon values on certain products went down, I hadn't paid more than a dime for toothpaste or a quarter for shampoo in thirty years. Conservatively speaking, during those years, at two tubes a month, I didn't pay more than seventy-two dollars for the 720 tubes of toothpaste my family likely used, versus the more than eight hundred dollars an average family would have paid in the same time period.

According to a 2007 study done by Debabrata (Debu) Talukdar, an associate professor of marketing, extreme cherry pickers make up only 1.2 percent of grocery store customers who are store hopping and purchasing only the loss leaders and sale items.

The missing category of coupon users: those who regularly leave stores with a cart full of merchandise they saved 80 to 90 percent on. They would most definitely be included in that extreme category, but would it be accurate to say they only buy the discounted items?

Some of us, like Lisa Erdmann of Pennsylvania, do fall squarely in this category. Lisa lives smack-dab in the middle of an area where there is fierce competition between grocery store chains like Weis, Landis, Acme, and Superfresh, resulting in frequent double-couponing events. Lisa does the majority of her shopping during those sales, stockpiling enormous amounts of free spaghetti sauce, pasta, condiments, and other non-perishables on shelves in her basement and meats and frozen foods in the three freezers in her house.

As for my grocery shopping opportunities, living in small town Iowa, outside of a few isolated doubling opportunities through the years, I am now limited to combining weekly sales and clearance-priced merchandise with the judicious use of coupons. Without doubling opportunities, I might stock up on ten jars of peanut butter when the price drops to one dollar a jar and I have "50¢ off" coupons, but there are plenty of occasions when I leave the store having spent one hundred dollars and (gasp!) used only a handful of coupons. My biggest savings is usually outside of the grocery store. Yet both Lisa and I identify ourselves as "Coupon Queens." Obviously, it isn't so easy to pigeonhole or differentiate between one saver and another.

An October 2012 *Business Insider* article looks at the four different kinds of savings addicts, including the "extreme couponer." The four types of ultimate savers included:

- The Tightwad, with the financial philosophy "It hurts to spend money."

- The Frugalist, with the philosophy "Saving money brings me joy."

- The Food Hoarders, with the philosophy "The more I buy, the more I save."

- The Extreme Couponer, "I enjoy getting more for less."

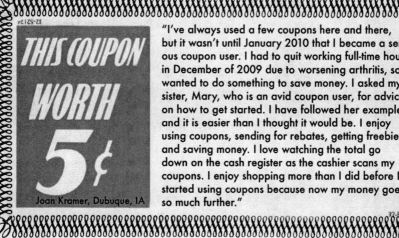

THIS COUPON WORTH 5¢

Joan Kramer, Dubuque, IA

"I've always used a few coupons here and there, but it wasn't until January 2010 that I became a serious coupon user. I had to quit working full-time hours in December of 2009 due to worsening arthritis, so I wanted to do something to save money. I asked my sister, Mary, who is an avid coupon user, for advice on how to get started. I have followed her example, and it is easier than I thought it would be. I enjoy using coupons, sending for rebates, getting freebies, and saving money. I love watching the total go down on the cash register as the cashier scans my coupons. I enjoy shopping more than I did before I started using coupons because now my money goes so much further."

Where did I fall in those categories? For years, it would have been squarely between the "extreme couponer" who bought anything that was free or cheap, whether she needed it or not, and the "food hoarder" with my huge stockpiles. My husband, however, was the avowed "Tightwad," rinsing out plastic storage bags and saving every disposable pie tin we ever used.

So, who exactly are the "Coupon Queens" of today? Is it even possible to pigeonhole this category of super savers?

We can get a general idea by looking at the specific trends of coupon use described by Nielsen:

- Affluent households tend to be the heaviest coupon users.

- Larger households tend to use more coupons.

- White households are more likely to be heavier coupon users.

- Hispanics and blacks are less likely to use coupons.

- Those with college degrees are more likely to use coupons.

Thanks to a lagging economy and the subsequent increase in coupon use and rapid advances in technology with Internet printed and cellphone coupons, the identity of the "Coupon Queen" is evolving, making it even more difficult to categorize them. For one thing, the "Queen" might actually be a "King." A May 2010 Harris Interactive poll conducted on behalf of Coupons.com revealed that 51 percent of adult males have used a coupon in the past six months, and over 36 percent of them actually have a designated place to keep their coupons.

Whoever we are—rich or poor, white or black, male or female—and whatever you want to call us—"cherry pickers," "coupon enthusiasts," "coupon commandoes," "shoptimizers," or just plain crazy—we do have something in common. We love a good deal, and we love talking about it.

When Trash
Was Cash

As the mother of two young children in the early 1980s I was convinced I was saving money by using cloth diapers. But by the time baby number three was born in 1987, I'd discovered a reward to using disposables. Besides the obvious convenience, the manufacturers of several brands were offering generous coupons as well as on-package points and proofs that could be mailed in for free toys, coupons, cash, and even savings bonds. I started taking walks with my children on trash day just to collect the extra proofs of purchase. We'd roam the alleys together, stopping at each diaper box. I learned to swiftly tear the proof of purchase off in a stealth maneuver I'd refined with practice: pushing the stroller up close to the box, bending down as if tying my shoe, and ripping off the qualifier, all in less than thirty seconds. The kids were eager to help, picking up candy wrappers or carrying the grocery sack we toted with us everywhere. They knew that picking up trash resulted in more Christmas gifts or checks Mom could cash in at the grocery store for the special treat I bought them for behaving while I shopped. Not only that, but our walks sometimes netted immediate satisfaction in the form of books, magazines, rolls of wrapping paper, or even toys that had been discarded. My two oldest children collected pop cans for the cash deposit they'd spend at the local candy store. Occasionally we even took a wagon with us to haul our bounty from our treks through the alleys.

One hot summer day when I was heavily pregnant with my fourth child, we hit the mother lode. As I peeled off the proofs of purchase from a group of several diaper boxes set out in the alley I heard a squeal of delight from my two-year-old, Michael. He'd peeked inside one of the boxes and discovered it was packed to the brim with toys! We looked inside the others and realized every single one was filled with Fisher Price Little People, Teenage Mutant Ninja Turtles, Lego pieces, and odds and ends of toys that suggested someone had cleaned out an entire playroom. We didn't have our wagon that day so we carried what we could the few blocks home, rushing back to get the remaining boxes. Just as we were about to pick them up, a woman appeared from around the corner of the garage, her arms crossed on her chest, her eyes narrowed to an angry slit.

"Get away from my garbage! That's my garbage."

Busted. I felt a hot blush spreading up to the roots of my hair. "My son saw the toys . . ." I started to say, my voice trailing off at her cold stare. We hastily retreated, our excitement sobered at her extreme reaction. That afternoon, the kids played with the selection of nearly new toys while I filed all the diaper proofs in my file cabinet.

Back then I had an entire room devoted to my hobby, with a desk, a huge shelf, and two file cabinets. The shelf displayed a dozen empty detergent boxes with the lids removed. Those detergent boxes held flattened boxes and larger labels. Some of the flattened boxes could be used several times for different offers; one offer might require a net weight statement, another a box top, and yet another, the box bottom, so the savvy refunder kept the entire box. The two file cabinets held the smaller labels and flattened medicine boxes. Whenever an offer came out, I could just go to my files and pull out the proofs of purchase I needed. And in the 80s and 90s, there was no end of offers. One of my 1991 refund bulletins listed eight hundred new offers that month alone.

The idea of filing one's trash is a foreign concept to the average consumer. Only those avidly participating in refunding

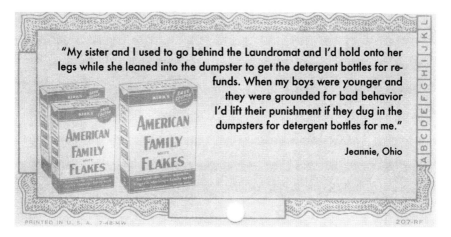

"My sister and I used to go behind the Laundromat and I'd hold onto her legs while she leaned into the dumpster to get the detergent bottles for refunds. When my boys were younger and they were grounded for bad behavior I'd lift their punishment if they dug in the dumpsters for detergent bottles for me."

Jeannie, Ohio

understood it. In fact, when a New York film crew visited my home in 1992 for a Whittle Communications report on couponing, they followed me around for hours asking questions about both couponing and refunding while filming me in my home and then as I shopped. In the Channel One edited video, narrated by celebrity Joan Lunden, only couponing is discussed. Included is a shot of me filing a Tylenol box in my file cabinet. I am sure more than one viewer wondered what saving medicine boxes had to do with using coupons.

Unfortunately for the companies offering the free premiums and cash incentives, the avid refunders did not behave in the way the companies hoped for. The intention, of course, was to encourage the consumer to purchase a particular product by offering an incentive, not to initiate alley walks and recycling center runs among housewives. Certainly there were times I bought extra Kraft Macaroni and Cheese specifically for the crayon offer or boxes of Fruit by the Foot for the personalized pencils, but for the majority of refunds, I simply went to my files to fulfill the offer. For many years, they made it easy for anyone willing to save their trash to participate in the offers on a grand scale. When Crest rewarded free AT&T gift certificates in exchange for UPCs from toothpaste boxes, I was able to pay my entire phone bill for several months with the boxes I'd already filed in my cabinet. I ordered a dozen strands of M&M lights with the candy bags a neighbor had saved for me. And every year, for several years in a row, Hershey outfitted my family with free T-shirts, thanks to the candy bar wrappers we'd collected from garbage cans. Yes, the years between 1970 and

1990 were a heyday for refunders. However, it wasn't long before companies caught on and began requesting dated cash register receipts or specially marked proofs of purchase.

VALUABLE CAMAY COUPON

REGULAR CAMAY FREE

YOUR DEALER WILL GIVE YOU

FREE

"My son was such a help with refunding. Once, on his way to school he saw a large Tide box in someone's garbage. He ran all the way back home with it, left it at the door, and ran all the way back to school because he didn't want to be late. He knew all the things I could get free and wanted to help!"

REGULAR CAMAY FREE

Sharon Johnson, WI

8300-BF

Like coupons, the concept of company premiums and refunds had been around for a while before I began participating in them in the 1980s. As early as 1851, B. T. Babbitt was offering color lithographs in exchange for their soap wrappers. It wasn't until ten years later that the company substituted coupons for the wrappers. And as mentioned previously in Chapter 3, it was in the 1880s that Adolphus Busch, a beer salesman from St. Louis, rewarded his favorite customers with a pocket knife. The gold knife with a corkscrew attached served as both a useful tool for barkeeps (beer was in corked bottles in the 1880s) as well as a reminder of both the product and the salesperson. In the handle of the pocket knife was a small glass dome with a picture of Adolphus inside. Busch seemed to have an innate understanding of the usefulness of promotions. Besides the knife, he distributed watch fobs, stick pins in the form of the company's A and Eagle trademark, and even playing cards, all in the name of promoting his beer.

According to a December 1971 *New York Times* article by James Nagle, the very first product premium offer might be traced as far back as 1793 when a merchant in Sudbury, New Hampshire gave away copper tokens that were redeemable for merchandise. Another early form of "trading" was implemented by Cyrus D. Jones, who started the Grand Union Tea Company in 1872. He gave out cardboard checks instead of tokens. The cardboard "tickets" could be collected and redeemed for premiums in a catalog.

As for trading stamps as we know them, they are a marketing tool that dates back to the late nineteenth and early twentieth century. According to Jeff R. Lont's three-part series, "The Trading Stamp Story," from Studio Z-7 Publishing, a department store in Milwaukee introduced the first trading stamps in 1891. Merchants would issue stamps to customers as an incentive to shop at their store. The gummed stamps were saved inside booklets that, when filled, could be exchanged for merchandise.

In 1896 the Sperry and Hutchinson Company became the first trading stamp company to operate as an independent business with their S&H Green Stamps. They provided stamps and booklets to merchants and even opened their own store where the only type of payment accepted was their own S&H stamp. Other companies and merchants soon followed suit, reaping billions of dollars by the mid-twentieth century. Stores and service stations handed out either S&H or other trading stamps to entice customers. Names like Gold Bond, Tripe-S, King Korn, Blue Chip, and Top Value popped up on the scene. By playing on a housewife's weakness for "free things" (sound familiar, avid couponers?) trading stamp books were one of the hottest sales ideas of the postwar decade. According to a 1995 *Time* magazine article, by the mid-1950s, over 100,000 United States retailers were using some form of stamp program to boost sales, and the US Department of Commerce estimated that stamp savers were redeeming their books for more than one billion dollars in premiums every year.

Stores that didn't offer trading stamps couldn't even begin to compete with the lure of "free stuff." When they attempted to do so by slashing prices, they ran the risk of a lawsuit. Safeway chain was slapped with an antitrust suit by the US Justice Department in 1957, and charged with selling goods below cost in order to compete against local stores that offered trading stamps. Well, if you can't beat them, join them. No longer able to compete by lowering prices, Safeway, A&P, and seven other chains and gasoline dealers formed the Blue Stamp Company, once again drawing the ire of the Justice Department. In 1963, they were charged with an antitrust suit for attempting to establish a trading stamp monopoly.

Trading stamp usage started to decline in the early 1970s and worsened when service stations dropped out of the programs during the gas shortage of the mid-1970s. Sperry & Hutchinson alone lost a quarter of its entire stamp business overnight. The last supermarket to give out the paper stamps was a Piggly Wiggly store in Columbia, Tennessee. That store finally gave them up in February 2003, leaving trading stamp books mostly a fond memory in the minds of the housewives who'd saved them. Surprisingly, Sperry & Hutchinson is still in business, with a modernized version of stamps, "greenpoints." No more licking and sticking, greenpoints are earned by shopping with the Sperry & Hutchinson card at participating grocery partners or online through their website. The points are accumulated and can be exchanged for gift cards to stores like Gap and Borders.

Grocery stores and gas stations weren't the only ones offering great deals. Naturally, cereal manufacturers that had been at the forefront in offering coupons on their products had to get in on the premium action too. Cereal makers began giving items such as spoons, cups, and even rag dolls either inside the boxes or through the mail with proofs of purchase. Kellogg's offered one of the first copyrighted novelty items in 1910, a Jungleland moving picture book. Children could interchange the cut-out sections of animal heads, bodies and legs in a six-page folder in the initial offer. Ralston cereal jumped on the bandwagon with radio show premiums like Tom Mix rings, badges, and toys that could be obtained with box tops.

Premium offers diminished in the 1940s when the United States went to war and basic goods became scarce and essentials rationed, but re-emerged in the early 1950s in a postwar economy that flourished. To appeal to the 1950s housewife, detergent and soap companies were prolific in their choice of premiums. Coverage of the New York Premium Show in a September 1963 issue of *The New York Times* mentions personalized notepads, dishes, spoons, and flatware, along with a send-in premium of a mink stole valued at $595. All a shopper had to do was mail in three wrappers from Underwood deviled ham to own it. Three wrappers and a check for $345, that is. In an eBay search for 1950s soap premiums I discovered a wide variety of dishes and flatware that had either been inside or attached to the box, or given free at the point of sale. In an era when televised soap operas were sponsored by detergent and soap companies (hence the name), homemakers sometimes found themselves choosing a certain brand of detergent just for the free towel or dishcloth included inside the box, just as their foremothers chose feed sacks for their color and design for future sewing projects.

Perhaps one of the more creative promotions of all time was in 1969, when a marketer with the Procter & Gamble Company came up with the idea of giving away goldfish with each purchase of a king-size box of Spic and Span. Rod Taylor relates in a June 2005 *Promo* magazine that planning the national promotion took over a year and called for more than a million goldfish. Once they devised a method of shipping the live fish to the stores in bags pumped full of oxygen, all systems were go for this innovative promotion. The promotion consisted of free-standing displays known as "nearpacks" (so called because they contained the premiums and were designed for display near the packs of detergent). Each nearpack came with plastic containers and even a net for scooping the fish out of the tank they were displayed in. Spic and Span's nearpack launch coincided with Proctor & Gamble's annual spring cleaning sale, with an early spring debut.

What the marketers hadn't counted on was the unpredictable weather. Goldfish shipped to Minnesota hit a cold snap and arrived frozen. Shipments to the Southwest hit an early heat wave

THIS COUPON **WORTH 15¢**

1 **GIANT SIZE**

In 1940, Hy-Vee found that customers were reluctant to use the newest "baskets on wheels," according to Dwight Vrendenburg in a February 20, 2000 "Des Moines Register" interview. Introduced in the Centerville, Iowa store, the grocery carts reminded women of baby buggies, and men thought the carts were for "sissies whose arms weren't strong enough to carry a few groceries." But a free candy bar in each new cart soon persuaded customers to try the new contraption.

Cash value 1/20th of 1 cent **COLGATE-PALMOLIVE-PEET CO., Jersey City, N. J.** 48-5224I

and were parboiled. Salespeople were called to stores all over to pick up dead fish and clean up messes from broken bags.

Promos and premiums weren't just for the consumer. The stores were often enticed to order more stock with what were called "dealer loaders," which were offered to a retailer for placing a larger than normal order. According to Rod Taylor in a June 2004 *Promo* magazine article, one of the earliest examples of loader premiums was executed by Old Town Canoe in 1915. Co-owner Sam Gray began giving a premium to dealers who ordered a full railcar of forty canoes. Their orders were rewarded with duplicates of the full-size canoes. Stores ordering eighty canoes could receive either two four-foot duplicates or one eight-foot model. The miniature canoe models were works of art in wood and canvas. Old Town used this strategy until around 1940.

A more recent prime example of promotions to retailers was the 1990 Procter & Gamble "O" gauge model train set offered to those who displayed at least 180 cases of four of the six sponsoring Proctor & Gamble brands, with over 15,000 stores participating. Each of the six cars in the set featured the logos of the sponsoring brands, including Folgers coffee, Sunny Delight, and Jif peanut butter. The store's logo and color was even printed on the train's locomotive.

One of the earliest marketing geniuses behind premium ploys was Sam Gold. An April 1949 *Life* magazine article called Gold the top idea man of the premium business. Born in 1900, Sam worked for Whitman Publishing Company in 1920, where he created and developed children's books. By 1922, he had moved to Chicago and started his own company, the American Advertising and Research Corporation. The corporation produced children's books along with premiums and displays. A maverick of his era, Sam believed that the world's greatest salesman was a child—able to sell to mom and dad. This concept was the principle foundation of his business. It was Sam Gold who went to the cereal companies with his marketing plans that included displays, posters, and radio scripts (later television) aimed at selling products to kids. He was soon known as the "Premium King," selling premiums to General Foods, Kellogg's, Quaker Oats, and other companies.

In the late 1940s, Gordon Gold, Sam's son, started his own company called Premium Specialties, where he designed a line of children's stock premiums that companies could purchase and have their name imprinted on. Gordon's company also produced character premiums such as Gene Autry buttons, rubber band guns, and Hopalong Cassidy badges.

In 1956, Gordon Gold and his father merged their companies and started another corporation, Gold Premiums of New York and Gold Manufacturing Corporation. Gordon became President of both companies while his father acted as vice-president. In 1957, Gordon Gold sold his first order to Nabisco cereal, an order of Rin-Tin-Tin telegraph key premiums.

TAKE THIS COUPON TO YOUR DEALER   5¢

"Sugar Crisp, the first sweetened cereal, was introduced in 1949 and began advertising on TV in the mid-1950s."

The Breakfast Cereal Gourmet,
by David Hoffman

5¢

Litho. in U.S.A. 11-57-G   Cash redemption value 1/20 of 1¢.   9526-XF

Sam Gold met his maker doing what he loved, dying in 1965 during a premium presentation to the Cracker Jack Company. His son ran the business until 1974 when he retired. In 1975, he presented his father's antique toy collection, the Gold Toy Collection, to the Museum of the City of New York.

Thanks in part to Gold's legacy of marketing to children, kids in the 1950s were the first generation to request cereal brands based on the premiums inside. Sales of Wheaties exploded in 1953 when they offered miniature license plates; and in 1969, legions of children like me demanded Cheerios for their breakfast, just because of the mail-in offer for a Super Ball. Children all over the United States were glued to the television screen, watching their favorite programs and being influenced by product sponsors. Television was an ideal forum, then and now, for sales pitches that involved children as a consumer base. Programs like *Howdy Doody* and *Andy's Gang* were closely identified with the brand that sponsored them. Ovaltine had kids mailing in labels for decoder badges, Ralston sponsored the *Tom Mix* decoder badge available in exchange for their box tops, General Mills sponsored *Lone Ranger* merchandise, and Rusty from *the Rin-Tin-Tin* show peddled other show-related premiums.

Of course, it was only a matter of time before fast-food chains wanted in on the premium rewards. Just two years after the McDonald's Happy Meal was introduced, a 1979 Star Wars-themed meal promotion included a series of comics based on the movie. Other fast-food chains mimicked that move, offering small toys with their children's meals. In 1996, McDonald's gained a major competitive advantage in the "movie tie-in premium wars" when it signed an agreement with Disney for exclusive rights to movie tie-in promotions for ten years.

Sam Gold was right about one thing: children are good sales-men—perhaps too good. You might say that today's children are

STORE COUPON

M-111

A campaign jingle from McDonald's in the 1980s: "Two-all-beef-patties-special-sauce-lettuce-cheese-pickles-onion-on-a-sesame-seed-bun." A special deal offered a free Coke if you could recite the entire jingle at the counter.

M-111

STORE COUPON

a marketer's best friend. According to a 2006 report from the Institute of Medicine, companies spend about seventeen billion dollars annually marketing to children. Not only that, children under fourteen spend about forty billion dollars annually and influence an additional five hundred billion dollars in purchases per year.

And while marketers might think that is great news, the general public—particularly parents—do not. A 2007 *Wall Street Journal* poll showed that 64 percent of people surveyed believe that popular characters should not be used to sell products to children. About half believe that marketing should be prohibited to children under the age of twelve.

Something Mr. Gold hadn't foreseen with his idea of marketing to youngsters was that all that television and all those premium promotions tied to junk food might result in a nation of fat children. Worry over our children's psyches and physical health has resulted in more and more restrictions put on marketers and advertisers. From the group "Campaign for a Commercial-Free Childhood," to the Federal Trade Commission's 2008 report, "Protecting America's Children," the consensus seems to be that children are influenced far too much by advertising, and if we can't eliminate it altogether, we should at least attempt to link premiums and promotions to good healthy food.

That is what Disney and Nickelodeon promised to do in 2006 in a move to tie their characters to lower-calorie foods. Disney included milk and fruit in the meals served at their theme parks, while Nickelodeon added popular character graphics on packages of fruit in 2007. Some high-ranking Disney officials also suggested that part of their company's decision not to renew the McDonald's exclusive movie tie-in contract was to put some distance between their company and the increasing obesity epidemic. This, despite the fact that McDonald's had already offered healthier choices of milk and apples to their children's menu and Disney continued to serve hamburgers and fries at their theme park. Fear of fat didn't stop DreamWorks Animation from signing a deal with McDonald's that year with promotions that tied in to the release of *Shrek 3*, but then what can we expect from a fat green ogre?

Premiums remain a popular form of promotion geared toward children, but more and more companies are shifting gears and business practices tying those promotions to healthier foods. In the fall of 2006, ten large food and beverage companies, including Kellogg's, vowed to strengthen their self-regulatory guidelines when marketing to children under the age of twelve. At least 50 percent of their ads would promote healthy food choices.

But what about the premiums and refunds geared to adults— the hundreds of new offers we used to see listed in our refund magazines every month? Now dubbed "rebates," they are fewer and farther between. For those of us involved in the game back then, all we have are fond memories of those days; or for women like Mary Grace Smith of Maryland, shelves full of collectible premium toys. Smith started collecting advertising premiums after she attended a presentation that discussed antiques and collectibles. When she returned home from the meeting, she noticed the Blue Bonnet Sue doll offer on the back of her margarine box. Enthused by the presentation she'd just witnessed, she sent for it, and the collection was launched. It wasn't long before she noticed all the refund premium offers in her Sunday coupon inserts. By the time she had obtained fifteen or twenty advertising toys through the mail, she began organizing her collection on a spreadsheet, noting dates, premium offers, and even copying the original refund form. When she and her husband moved in 2003, they packed up several display cases and nearly 200 collectible "toys" to go along with them. Smith especially liked premiums unique to the product; the Tidy Cat, the Raid Bug, the Kodak Colorkin stuffed animals, and the Fischer Sandwich Mouse, to name a few. My personal favorites were the Energizer Bunny premiums, a series of Rudolph reindeers with glowing noses from the Duracell Company, and Del Monte vegetable and fruit-themed "Yumkin" stuffed animals and Christmas ornaments that adorn my tree to this day. My children have fond memories of all the soccer balls, baseballs, toy cars, and shirts emblazoned with candy bar decals.

As I've gathered information from couponers and former refunders throughout the United States, I was reminded of good deals I'd forgotten about and others I hadn't even been aware of.

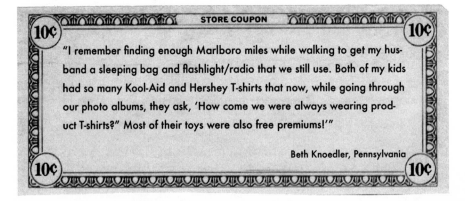

Gathering those stories and quotes became more than a trip down memory lane for me. It reminded me of how much couponing and refunding has meant to me throughout the years, and how I always felt a part of something much bigger than myself—a cultural phenomenon and an entire community of coupon users.

6¢

The Coupon Community

I loved writing term papers and research papers in high school. I was one of the few students who actually preferred essay tests. I learned the rudimentary skills of conducting research at the hands of a high school teacher who took us to a college library to show us how to seek out answers to our questions. Later, beginning classes at that same college, I already knew where the green *Reader's Guide to Periodicals* were located and became a pro at reading news articles on microfilm and microfiche (I know, I'm really dating myself). As an undergraduate, I was required to take a class in statistics where we typed our facts and figures into a machine that transformed them into a stack of cards with holes punched into them. These punch cards were then fed into a computer that filled an entire room.

Fast forward to the summer of 2006: My husband was just diagnosed with oral cancer, and I found myself, once again, doing research. This time, in front of a desktop computer. I was amazed at the ease and speed that I was able to obtain information.

So it has been in researching the science of shopping and the history of coupon use. Everything I wanted to know was just a mouse click away. Not just that, but I already had a built-in community of avid couponers and former refunders to interview. They were the consumers in the trenches of the grocery store aisles with their coupon binders and boxes, the ones who intimately knew the "high" that could be had from a good deal. As I delved deeper, I posted calls for submissions on websites like RefundCents.com and HotCouponWorld.com, and I discovered that not only did my fellow couponers enjoy saving money, but they loved talking about it as well. This was not unexpected. In several research studies, the conclusion was that the "super savers" differed from the average shopper with their extreme enthusiasm in talking about their deals, a phenomenon my friends and family can attest to regarding my own super shopping trips.

Long before the ease of networking via the Internet, I was avidly pursuing like-minded women for support as a stay-at-home mom. In one town, it was morning coffee at a friend's house while our children played together. In another, where my husband took master's courses at the university, my new friend Mary introduced me to a weekly playgroup at her church. And there were always magazines like the now-defunct *Women's Circle* where I could choose pen-pals with similar interests.

So it was in connecting with other couponers. In the 1980s and early 1990s, refunding and couponing magazines proliferated. At one time I subscribed to several: *Refundle Bundle, Moneytalk, Refund Express, and Refunding Makes Cents.* Each would arrive in my mailbox on a different day of the month, and I could usually pay for my subscriptions by writing articles or by being the first to send in a new form for credit. As a stay-at-home mom of several young children, I struggled to make ends meet. Couponing and refunding allowed me to stretch my budget, but like most stay-at-home moms, I often felt isolated. Trading with other couponers meant that not only did I share a sense of community with others who were like me, but that I could cash in on even more offers with the forms and coupons I traded for. As mentioned earlier, there was a point when I was trading through the mail with fourteen other women. Those envelopes full of letters, coupons, proofs of purchase, and refund forms were like treasures in my mailbox. The women I traded with were spread out all over the country, ensuring that I had access to rebate forms and coupons widely distributed in other states but not available in Iowa.

Besides trading through the mail in response to ads in the bulletins, women all over the nation were conducting "refund conventions," and "coupon swaps"—meeting at someone's house or in a public meeting room and trading coupons and refund forms with each other, a practice I'd heard about but never had the opportunity to participate in.

The section of the refunding magazines I found the most fascinating were the profiles of subscribers and their stories, written by

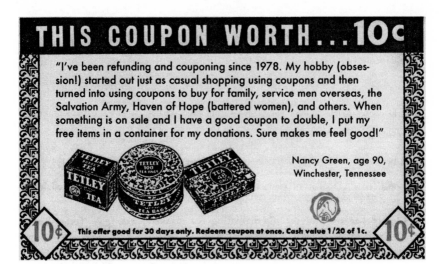

other people who were also crazy about coupons. I experienced a real sense of community, and some envy, in reading about the toy deal of a lifetime or someone's recent savings on diapers. Pictures of subscribers with their stacks of free boxes of crackers, carefully arranged bottles of shampoos, and babies nestled in their car seats surrounded by a mountain of free formula or diapers, left me with a feeling of kinship, as if we were all one big family participating in the same fun hobby. Every day my mailbox was full of letters and thick envelopes stuffed with coupons. I impatiently waited for the refund magazines to arrive so I could see what new offers were out or what the current hot coupon was that I might not have gotten in my own coupon inserts, but could trade for.

Enter the era of the Internet, and the end of the waiting game.

I didn't jump on the Internet bandwagon until 1998. At that time I was helping my husband get a bookstore off the ground, as well as selling books to homeschoolers through a list I mailed out every six weeks. I'd noticed that several vintage children's books were a hot commodity among my clients. Books by authors such as Lois Lenski, Maud Hart Lovelace, Lenora Mattingly Weber, and Janet Lambert were snatched up so quickly that I couldn't keep them in stock. One of my customers, a homeschooling mother from New York, telephoned me every month with her long order. The first thing I did when I got online was to peruse the auction site I'd heard mentioned by other booksellers—eBay. It only took me a few minutes to discern that my top-buyer was selling the very books I'd sold her, for ten times the price!

The second thing I did, after signing up for my own eBay account, was to investigate the websites of my two favorite refund magazines. The message boards and forums introduced me to a whole new world of shopping, with an instant access and immediate notification of deals, both in the stores and online. Unfortunately for my budget, I temporarily became a marketer's best friend, ripe for the picking as an isolated, homeschooling mother of six. I was particularly vulnerable to the peer pressure environment of a refunding website where everyone raved about that day's "good deals" on the boards—something I'd never encountered with a monthly magazine—where the majority of the deals were already over by the time I'd read about them. Suddenly I had instant access to good deals. I could read about a product being clearanced on the shelves of a chain store in the morning and rush to the nearest one that very afternoon to see if our area was having the same deal. I'd hear through the group grapevine the timing of Target's after-Christmas "75% off" sale and, with kids in tow, head there an hour before it opened so I could be first in line for the drastically discounted Christmas decorations, paper, perfume sets, and holiday flannel sheet sets. As for the online offers, I'm afraid I succumbed to the hype for a few months, as I pulled out my brand new charge card to cover the handling fees and shipping charges on the many new customer introductory code offers. The small charges added up rapidly, and I actually felt a little sick to my stomach the day the UPS truck delivered two Rubbermaid toy boxes and three laundry baskets from a deal that seemed too good to pass up. (On a side note, those toy boxes went through thirteen years and three children intact, so perhaps they really did constitute a good deal.) I abruptly came to my senses one day when I found myself considering the purchase of ten drastically-reduced cashmere sweaters—I don't even wear sweaters!

"Can you believe it? Ninety percent off, and free shipping when you order ten!" my couponing peers raved about the Macy's special on a coupon forum board. I was amazed by the dramatic savings, but it had taken at least three months of indiscriminate spending to make me realize I wasn't saving anything at all, buying things I didn't need just because my deal-seeking peers were.

I had to quit cold turkey—at least until I was pregnant with my seventh child and hell-bent on ordering some high-end boutique quality blankets with yet another introductory offer. With a special "$20 code" offered to new customers, I would get a generous twenty dollars' worth of merchandise free. I learned to use my husband's name and e-mail address for an additional order since most of the offers were one per customer, and my husband could be considered a separate customer. With these special introductory offers, I enjoyed free baby clothes and receiving blankets that were delivered right to my door, along with huge discounts on a much-needed (unlike the cashmere sweaters) high chair and car seat.

I didn't have to rely on my own Internet surfing to discover these special offers, either. It seemed like a new website popped up every day that would do all the legwork for me—alerting consumers to new sales and special discount code offers that were updated frequently throughout the day. While there are still the occasional free sample or introductory special prices offered today, the landscape of freebie offers is nothing like what I experienced during my first two years online. Now, the offers can morph and disappear from one hour to the next, meaning anyone who is intent on taking advantage of them has to be checking the deal-seeking sites quite frequently.

THIS COUPON WORTH 10¢

48-53009

"It began as a sort of hobby. I wasn't very serious, but I did get the idea that by using coupons and sales at the grocery store, I could save a bunch. As our family grew, saving money with coupons became a part-time job. Now I absolutely delight in the savings. My husband thinks I'm slightly nuts, but if he only knew how much I've saved over the years—probably thousands of dollars."

Pam Pierre, Minnetonka, Minnesota

Cash value 1/20th of 1 cent   COLGATE-PALMOLIVE-PEET CO., Jersey City 2, N. J.

Wondering what coupons will come out next Sunday? Wonder no longer. Shoppers don't have to wait until the Sunday newspaper arrives to see what coupons will be inside. There are websites that list those inserts ahead of time. Looking for extra coupons? For a handling fee, another website might offer a coupon clipping service where you can choose which coupons you'd like mailed to you. And if you want to find the best price on toilet paper, there are websites that will list the weekly sales of major grocery store and discount chains. Need shoes? You can visit one website that will show you where to find your favorite brand discounted and another that will give you online codes to type into the promo code area for an additional discount on top of that. Go through a website like Ebates.com or ShopAtHome.com for a rebate on a percentage of your online spending at participating stores.

The old coupon community that existed in the monthly bulletins or magazines has either become obsolete or moved online too, offering forums for good deal alerts and discussions on topics ranging from the correct use of coupons to tips on how to deal with an irate cashier. One of these websites, RefundCents.com,

TAKE THIS LEVER COUPON TO YOUR DEALER

6¢

COUPON
toward
purchase of
1 pound

"The thing I love most about couponing is looking in my wallet at all those smiling faces I've saved! (Andrew Jackson, Alexander Hamilton, Abraham Lincoln)"

— Tony Irvin,
Chattanooga, Tennessee

includes an off-topic forum where members can discuss anything from cancer scares to potty-training tips. Once again, I can experience that nostalgic feeling of camaraderie, a sense of being part of a frugal family.

Looking at audience profiles for websites such as RefundCents. com can give an idea of how many and what type of people are interested in coupon savings. In September of 2007, when I was initially considering writing about this subject, I checked reports from Quantcast for an audience profile for RefundCents.com. At that time, RefundCents.com ranked 92,189 among 202,679,777 websites studied and reached approximately 16,363 monthly, unique, US viewers. The site drew a more educated, mostly Caucasian, predominately female, and older audience. As noted in previous research and studies, the predominant household income of site viewers was between $30,000 and $60,000, with the over $100,000 income group coming in a close second.

Interestingly, by March of 2010, this same site ranked 40,820 and reached approximately 40,000 unique viewers. The demographics of race, age, and income remained about the same. This increase in viewership and ranking likely reflected the downturn in the economy and the increased interest in couponing in those three years.

Another website that analyzes website traffic, Compete. com, reported 52,220 unique visitors for RefundCents in April 2010. WeUseCoupons.com went from 80,906 unique visitors in April 2010 to 156,866 in January 2011. Stephanie Nelson, of CouponMom fame, boasted an extraordinary 992,229 unique visitors in January of 2011, proving that a large segment of the population is indeed interested in saving more at the grocery store with coupons.

Despite the fact that men do use coupons, there is still a gender difference; according to an ongoing survey of women conducted and commissioned by Fleishman-Hillard and Hearst magazines, women outpace men by 10 to 20 percentage points on most measures. The study, "Women, Power & Money," set out to examine today's successful woman and concluded that women had become the de facto CEO of most American households. The fourth wave of the study, released in January 2012, titled "Game

"Women, who comprise just over 51 percent of the US population, control six trillion dollars in buying power annually, according to the Bureau of Economic Analysis."

Pocketbook Power,
by Bernice Kanner

Changers: Women Defining the New American Marketplace," found that a woman's preferences have amplified and become the de facto defining preferences for today's marketplace. The emergence of social media, which "expands one's sphere of influence, and has shaped the attitude that one can and should express opinions," has been instrumental in increasing a woman's influence in the marketplace. For instance, women are more likely than men to be a friend or fan of a product or company on Facebook. The article concluded that the proliferation of information in the marketplace, the economic downturn, and the emergence of social media has made the market ripe for coupons and discounts and fostered a fundamental shift in marketplace power.

There is no denying that technology plays a huge role in the lives of today's women, especially mothers. My *Women's Circle* magazine with the recipes and pen pal ads has been replaced by the social media of Facebook, Twitter, and blogs. BSM Media's research indicates that two in three (65%) of today's moms use at least five separate technologies, including wireless devices, videos, and blogs, just to get through their days. According to Quantcast, 42 million American women take part weekly in social media, and 76 percent of women between the ages of eighteen and twenty-six regularly engage in social media.

The Nielsen Company, which tracks consumer trends and behavior around the world, reports that 87 million American women between the ages of eighteen and seventy-six go online (with 68 million using social media) at least once a week, and that blogs are twice as likely as social networks to be used to learn about new trends, ideas, and products.

Companies are carefully studying the influence of the increasingly popular blogs. With nearly 80,000 new blogs launching every day, marketers are looking for those bloggers who are the most influential in regards to recommending products and services. A public relations firm such as Access Communications can help companies decide which bloggers have the most influence in the world of the Web. Access Blog Influence Engine (ABIE), a web-based application that provides an accurate, comprehensive view of true influence on the web, can also offer a clearer insight into how to foster stronger blogger relationships. ABIE contains ranked

4632BN
12796

TAKE THIS COUPON TO YOUR STORE

Babble.com's Top Ten Bloggers in 2012

- The Bloggess
- Moosh in Indy
- Design Mom
- Dooce
- Girls Gone Child
- Black and Married With Kids

- Mom 101
- Momastery
- Motherlode
- Edenland

10¢

10¢

12796

lists of dozens of categories of blogs, including detailed profiles of more than 5,000 of the most influential bloggers.

Ilana Westerman, CEO and co-founder of Create with Context, a digital stragety consulting practice, and Elisa Camahort Page, cofounder of BlogHer, studied women shoppers in their "Women, the Web, and Their Wallets" study. They determined that 35 percent of women trust a product review from a blogger more than any user reviews on company websites. According to Quantcast, about 23 million American women are weekly readers or contributors to blogs.

Estimates of the "mommy blogger" population in the United States range from 1.8 million all the way up to 3.3 million. A survey by the Nielsen Company found that so-called "Power Moms," ages twenty-five to fifty-four and with at least one child, represent 20 percent of the active online population. Their universal concern? Money. Within that blogger segment, composed of more than 10,000 parenting and mom-oriented blogs, Nielsen found an increasing concern about the economy, with savvy

Internet shoppers scouring for money-saving strategies and good deals. There are plenty of "Mom Blogs" to choose from. Chiefmarketer.com demographics estimates there were 26 million mommy bloggers in April 2010. From family to fashion, fun, and finance, moms account for 2 trillion dollars worth of purchases annually, a fact that has advertisers scrambling to reach them as an audience.

A Chicago-based agency, Fuor Digital, recently uncovered key insights and statistics to help their clients understand the new "digital mom." Moms with very young children are at least 50 percent more likely than the average online American to create social content and join online communities. With over half of mothers reading blogs, marketers have found yet another niche for advertising and promotion. Moms have always had a huge influence on the marketplace but the new frugality spurred by a rising unemployment rate, housing woes, and rising food prices has increased the flow of traffic on websites such as Couponmom. com, one of the five most influential mom blogs of the 10,000 parenting blogs studied by Nielsen. Coupon mom Stephanie Nelson attracted 972,000 unique visitors in March of 2009, five times more than just a year earlier. There is no doubt that people are searching the Internet for ways to save money and other purchasing decisions.

According to a Forbes report on mom bloggers, the top fifteen mom bloggers influence more people than the *New York Times* newspaper. Brands are wise to partner with some of these influential bloggers.

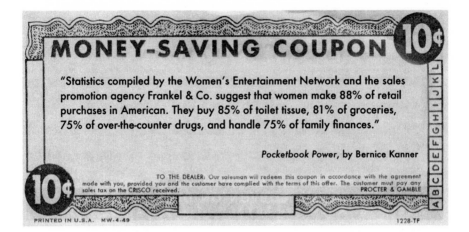

MONEY-SAVING COUPON **10¢**

"Statistics compiled by the Women's Entertainment Network and the sales promotion agency Frankel & Co. suggest that women make 88% of retail purchases in American. They buy 85% of toilet tissue, 81% of groceries, 75% of over-the-counter drugs, and handle 75% of family finances."

Pocketbook Power, by Bernice Kanner

TO THE DEALER: Our salesman will redeem this coupon in accordance with the agreement made with you, provided you and the customer have complied with the terms of this offer. The customer must pay any sales tax on the CRISCO received.   PROCTER & GAMBLE

PRINTED IN U.S.A.   MW-4-49   1228-TF

Retailers and consumer product makers have definitely taken note of the influence of these mom-oriented blogs. Companies like Frigidaire and Unilever will give free samples of their merchandise to key mom bloggers to test and chat about on their sites. In 2008, Walmart Stores, Inc. joined the fray by creating an entire online community, elevenmoms.com, on its website. They spotlight women bloggers like dealseekingmom.com, couponcravings.com, beingfrugal.com, and consumerqueen.com. While Walmart does not pay the women to review their products, it does offer them products for free to review.

Of course, the Federal Trade Commission (FTC) has had something to say about this. So-called "sponsored posts" are considered an extension of traditional advertising and public relations. The FTC revised its guidelines in 2009 for product testimonials and endorsements. Social media marketing can be a sticky issue because of the difficulty of distinguishing between a casual mention of a product and a paid product placement. In order to comply with FTC regulations, bloggers have to disclose that the reviewed product was given to them.

Even casual mentions on my blog of a particular brand of toy that my children were obsessed with actually attracted the attention of a representative of that company. Her job was to google their company name, looking for influential bloggers to do reviews. After her Google search lead her to my blog twice in four months, she contacted me, asking if I'd like to review some of their newest toys. She didn't have to ask me twice. Free toys? I couldn't help but have a flashback to the diaper boxes full of toys my children and I had carted home from someone's garbage years before. This time I didn't have to have my dignity assaulted or get my hands dirty in the alley. Instead, a small box arrived on my doorstep, and my children dutifully played with the toys while I listened and observed. They weren't thrilled with the turtle that was included, but they loved the other animals. We were able to keep the toys, and all I had to do was agree to disclose that the company had sent them. It wasn't a refrigerator or a washer/dryer combo, but if some company wants to send me one of those, I'd be happy to do the same thing for them.

While it is obvious that the Internet and social media has had a big impact in the life of deal-seekers and coupon users, unfortunately it has also served to increase and diversify coupon fraud, as we'll see in the next chapter.

Stop Thief!
Drop That
Coupon

"I couldn't bother to take the time to use coupons. It's just pennies," a friend once commented. At the time, I was regularly saving thirty dollars a week on my grocery bill, an amazing three thousand pennies a week.

Coupons really were worth only a few pennies in the 1950s and 1960s, with average face values of five to twenty cents, hardly "big money" even then. Yet in skimming through newspaper archives, I came across an August 27, 1951, *New York Times* article estimating illegal cashing in of coupons to be a million dollars a year. One of the largest swindles reported was in early 1950 when a company sent out 1,000,000 postcards that offered housewives in the metropolitan area free tea bags, with a redemption value of 21 cents. A letter carrier in Brooklyn stole the cards, sold them to a news dealer for 8 cents each, who in turn sold them to a grocer for 9 cents each. That grocer sold the cards to fellow grocers for 13 cents each. Seems like an awful lot of trouble to make a few pennies. The wholesaler who was reimbursing the grocers to the tune of 21 cents each for boxes of tea bags that hadn't even been sold lost fifty thousand dollars before the illegal scheme was revealed. Just thirteen years later, eight men were indicted in Brooklyn for illicitly obtaining and selling coupons to the tune of one hundred thousand dollars.

Just pennies? That's an awful lot of pennies! And with the face value of coupons increasing every year, the potential for fraudulent redemption and counterfeit coupons has increased as well.

According to a CPGMatters August 2012 report, Inmar has seen submissions of counterfeit coupons increase by more than 20 percent in the first half of 2012. "Counterfeiters are getting more aggressive and more sophisticated, making it more and more difficult for cashiers to stop this fraud at the point of sale," Matthew Tilley, director of Marketing of Inmar Promotion Network was quoted as saying.

Advancing technology has brought some solutions to identifying counterfeit coupons. Besides the new GS1 Data Bar and the ability to serialize coupons, the Coupon Information Center (CIC), a nonprofit association founded to encourage integrity in connection with the redemption of manufacturer's coupons, offers a hologram that can be printed on coupons and an early warning system for retailers and CIC members. Known counterfeit coupons are also posted on the CIC website.

As I perused archives from as far back as 2003, I was shocked to see one of the counterfeit coupons listed was for a free package of Twizzlers licorice. Why? Because in the late 1990s I'd used several free Twizzlers coupons a woman had sent me in response to an ad I'd run in a refund bulletin. Had I used a fraudulent coupon? If a thirty-year veteran of the coupon world had been so easily fooled by a bogus coupon, how could a less-experienced cashier or coupon user know the difference between a genuine and a fake?

That epiphany finally led me to take another look at coupon fraud and how it applied to my own couponing practices. Evidently, I had inadvertently used at least one, and perhaps more, counterfeit coupons in my time.

Monitoring for fake coupons is something that Bud Miller, Executive Director of the Coupon Information Corporation (CIC) can spend a good portion of his day doing. In the six months after December 2009, his organization discovered 250 fake coupons, more than the previous decade combined. What does his agency do once they identify the counterfeit coupons? Miller emails food makers and retailers and posts alerts on popular couponing web-sites, as well as the CIC website, www.couponinformationcenter. com. In the month of May 2011 alone, there were twenty-five new counterfeit coupons posted on the CIC website.

Today, if you do a Google search for "coupon fraud" on the Internet, Bud Miller is one of the two names that inevitably appears; Jill Cataldo is the other. You can read dozens of state-ments attributed to Mr. Miller in the newspaper archives where he repeatedly contends that the only place a consumer should obtain coupons is from the newspapers they themselves buy off the stands. In other words, there should be no trading or purchasing of extra coupons.

Back in my couponing and refunding days, when I traded coupons and forms with women all over the country, I couldn't fathom Mr. Miller's hardline stance on coupon trading. Where was the harm? Later, when I got online and began ordering some extra coupons through the mail, I heard that Bud Miller wanted to see eBay and coupon handling websites suspend coupon sales altogether. He was often quoted as saying, "There is no legitimate reason to buy coupons." Really? I couldn't imagine that he was a couponer. Surely an avid couponer would understand the need for extra coupons when imbibing in healthy stockpiling.

Jill Cataldo, however, is an avid coupon user. Cataldo—consumer advocate, coupon workshop instructor, and syndicated newspaper columnist—is a self-professed coupon maven. She has also become a voice of reason in the otherwise volatile world of "extreme couponing" and a vocal proponent of couponing ethics.

Through my extensive research, I've gradually, and somewhat reluctantly, come to the conclusion that Miller and Cataldo have a valid concern in regards to at least one of the various methods couponers employ in obtaining additional coupons: purchasing them through the mail, through websites like eBay, or coupon handling websites that offer a "clipping service." "It's a violation of the terms and conditions printed right there on the coupon," Bud Miller said in a Tampa Bay online article.

Keeping in mind that I used to be one of the couponers who retrieved stray coupon inserts from a recycling center, it should come as no surprise that I'd also utilized coupon clipping services on occasion, albeit services from a source I knew and trusted. And yes, I'd also purchase extra coupons on eBay. Neither of these methods is technically illegal—yet. Avid couponers like me definitely can see a legitimate reason to obtain more coupons than those received in our own Sunday newspaper. How else can we stockpile peanut butter when it goes on sale for one dollar with a one dollar coupon available? Buying additional newspapers is an option I often employ, but I also depend on friends and family members to share their unwanted inserts with me.

Unfortunately, or fortunately (depending upon how you look at it), after intensively researching coupon fraud, I have become a convert to the idea of banning all coupon sales. Why? Because I've gotten a glimpse into the dark underbelly of the coupon world, and it isn't pretty.

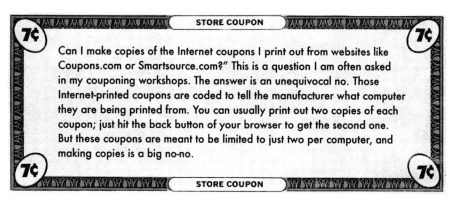

STORE COUPON

Can I make copies of the Internet coupons I print out from websites like Coupons.com or Smartsource.com?" This is a question I am often asked in my couponing workshops. The answer is an unequivocal no. Those Internet-printed coupons are coded to tell the manufacturer what computer they are being printed from. You can usually print out two copies of each coupon; just hit the back button of your browser to get the second one. But these coupons are meant to be limited to just two per computer, and making copies is a big no-no.

STORE COUPON

It was way too easy for me to unearth counterfeit coupons listed on eBay just by doing a search under "free coupon." I discovered dozens of listings of coupons for free products, sold by sellers whose selling history I scrutinized carefully. There is absolutely no legitimate method of obtaining as many free product coupons as these sellers were listing, not even if they'd written hundreds of complaint letters to companies and received free coupons in return. As for the clipping services, until I scrutinized the fine print on the majority of coupons, I'd never considered that a concern. After all, these were legitimate manufacturer coupons and buyers weren't being charged for the coupons, but the service of the clipping. Except, if that is true, why is a buyer charged more for a $5 coupon than a 50¢ coupon? If the fine print on the coupon states that it isn't allowed to be sold, it's hard to rationalize that pricing. I've had to adjust my purchasing and stockpiling somewhat since I've abandoned the purchase of extra coupons, but I still manage to stockpile things my family uses on a regular basis, through the strategic combination of sale prices, clearance prices, and coupon clipping.

Bud Miller has seen it all in regards to coupon fraud, and it goes way beyond a consumer trying to purchase a quart-sized product with the specified gallon-sized coupon. Miller's agency has been at the forefront of some of the biggest coupon-fraud sting operations in history.

Let's back up a bit and distinguish the difference between coupon fraud and coupon misredemption. According to CPGMatters.com, *fraud* is the broadest term, encompassing mis/malredemption and counterfeiting. Misredemption can include activities like a retailer mailing bogus coupons with authentic ones when submitting them, or falsifying an invoice. Malredemption can occur when a consumer purposely misuses the terms of an offer by not purchasing the specifically promoted brand.

For the purpose of this chapter, I look at coupon fraud as a multi-million dollar criminal activity and an intentional illegal practice that includes counterfeiting, wholesale trading or brokering, and submissions from a non-existent retail operation. Misredemption, or malredemption, would then include the intentional violation of coupon policies, such as retailers accepting expired coupons and allowing alternate product purchases for customers or a consumer purposely redeeming a coupon with the intention of obtaining a product of a different size than specified on the coupon or even a different product. That would be an intentional misredemption, and one that the majority of my couponing peers would frown upon, but that has actually been encouraged on some message boards.

Just how prevalent is coupon fraud, and how long has it been a problem? In December of 1977, the CFCP Company introduced Breen detergent to the New York market. Their introductory 25¢ coupon, delivered via a free-standing insert, saw a 2.5 percent redemption rate, translating to more than 70,000 first-time users of Breen. The only problem: there was no detergent named Breen. CFCP stood for Coupon Fraud Control Program, and every coupon redeemed was for a product that didn't exist from a manufacturer that also didn't exist.

In August of that year, the US Postal Service asked Blair Marketing to create a sting operation that would catch crooks without disrupting legitimate redemption. The bogus detergent was at the center of the first major coupon fraud offensive in US history. On December 11, 1977, editions of the *Daily News*, *Newsday*, and *Newark Star Ledger* all carried the Breen coupon. None of the newspapers knew they were running a fake coupon, but the firms that submitted it had to have known they were guilty of misredemption since no such brand existed and they couldn't possibly have sold it.

As a result of the sting operation, twenty-six retailers were indicted by the Brooklyn District Attorney on charges ranging from scheming to defraud to grand larceny. Four of the retailers were charged exclusively for their actions in fraudulently redeeming the Breen coupon, having submitted from 24,000 to 117,000 of them.

That sting and others since then have revealed several forms of coupon fraud:

- Individuals or groups submitting coupons using fake store fronts and multiple business names.

- Legitimate retailers "padding" their own submissions of coupons, redeeming coupons as having gone through their own tills without actually having sold those items.

- Coupon brokers who steal, buy, and sell coupons to make money.

- Coupon rings or scams, involving counterfeit coupons.

The widespread fraudulent redemption of that one detergent coupon forced major companies to re-evaluate coupon production.

They began using technology that consecutively numbered each coupon as it was printed so retailers submitting batches with too many consecutive numbers could be added to a "coupon watch" list by marketers.

The coupon watch system has been instrumental in many indictments since then. Federal investigators have teamed up with postal inspectors to uncover coupon rings and fraud. In 1986, a Miami-based ring was uncovered that had bilked approximately $186 million from companies nationwide. A bogus bug spray coupon was at the center of the SWAT team bust. When approximately fifty South Florida grocery store operators showed up at Sheraton River House near the Miami International Airport, they expected to collect money for coupons they claimed to have cashed for customers. Instead, they were greeted by one hundred law enforcement officials. In a *Sun Sentinel* article about the sting, Miami chief postal inspector Mark Grey claimed that members of the ring either purchased or stole tens of thousands of coupons and then shipped them to clearinghouses on behalf of grocery retailers.

More than fifty-five million dollars in coupon-related fraud was uncovered in Pennsylvania alone between 1982 and 1987.

The "Al Capone" of coupon misredemption in the 1980s had to be Larry Krasnick, the ring-leader of a forty-four million dollars coupon ring. Krasnick recruited small store owners, who had redeemed very few coupons before they met him. Suddenly, they were redeeming thousands of coupons, and Krasnick's crime syndicate was helping them process those coupons for payment.

As Krasnick's business grew larger, he set up phony storefronts exclusively for the purpose of misredeeming coupons. And where did all those coupons come from? Krasnick estimated that of the 110 million coupons he misredeemed over a period of ten years, 99.9 percent came from non-profit groups.

Yes, charity groups. In a 1997 interview, US Postal Inspector Rick Bowden stated that religious or charitable organizations were the unwitting suppliers of coupons in almost every major coupon-fraud investigation he'd conducted in the previous twenty years. In 1997, more than 90 percent of the coupons run through the stream of fraudulent misredemption were clipped by very nice people who thought they were helping the poor, children with cancer, private religious schools, or whatever cause they donated the money to. Instead, they were unwitting accomplices to the crime of coupon misredemption.

Coupon crooks can get pretty creative in obtaining extra coupons to run through the system. According to a 1988 *Los Angeles Times* article in 1972, a Los Angeles accountant recruited hundreds of housewives to clip newspaper coupons, paying them $5 a pound. A few years later, authorities discovered a "cutting room" in the Northern California community of San Bruno, staffed entirely by illegal aliens who were being paid one to two cents for every coupon they clipped.

In a more recent coupon fraud case, in March of 2007, seven men pled guilty for their roles in a New Jersey–based, multi-state coupon redemption fraud scheme. The defendants admitted that between October 1999 and July 2004 they'd contacted at least fifty-four stores and retail outlets in New Jersey, New York, Pennsylvania, and Maryland, soliciting participation in a coupon redemption promotion which would qualify the store owners to receive cash payments by redeeming manufacturer coupons through doctored applications to clearinghouses. The defendants submitted tens of thousands of coupons to clearinghouses that issued checks totaling more than $580,000 to the store owners, who would then pay 50 percent or more of the money to the masterminds of the criminal activity.

It isn't just the grocery stores and the coupon brokers who have been busted for coupon fraud. Fraud even infiltrated one of the coupon clearinghouses. Coupon clearinghouses have been around since 1957, collecting coupons from the stores, submitting them to the issuing companies for reimbursement, and then redistributing that money to the retailers. Their income comes through handling fees and other charges.

Robert MacDonald, also known as "Big Mac" worked for one of the biggest clearinghouses in the United States: International Outsourcing Services (IOS), a company that in 2007 employed five thousand people nationwide, with a corporate office in West El Paso. As the Memphis office manager in 2004, MacDonald was convicted for stealing more than $50 million by way of coupon fraud. What he didn't pocket himself went to support groups with alleged ties to terrorism.

Eleven individuals employed by IOS were indicted in federal court in March 2007 for the alleged nine-year 250 million dollar fraud against packaged-goods marketers. The center allegedly used a cement mixer in Mexico to make coupons that had never gone through store's tills appear to have been handled. By April of 2012, four of the eleven defendants named in the indictment had pled guilty. The case has yet to be brought to trial.

A request to have the eventual trial moved from Milwaukee to El Paso was denied by the judge on the case. US Magistrate Judge Patricia Gorence stated in her ruling that "*this factor* weighs against the transfer of venue." What was the overriding factor mentioned in the ruling? It was ten tons of evidence, most of it coupons, stored in a warehouse near Milwaukee. Yes, you read that correctly: *ten tons of coupons.* I can hear the collective gasp now—of jealousy, not dismay—from avid couponer readers. Too bad the coupons would all be expired by now.

In these cases, the coupons were actually legitimate, unlike the Breen coupon sting. But what about counterfeit coupons? Just as marketers took advantage of newer technology in numbering and coding their coupons, so did scam artists, particularly those dealing in counterfeit coupons.

In the late 1980s coupon counterfeiters got so sophisticated in making their phony coupons that they were able to produce coupons that looked identical to the original coupons issued by the companies. Coupons—valued from $1 to $20, for anything from free batteries to bags of Doritos—were copied and distributed by racketeers in the phony coupon business. If a manufacturer had offered a legitimate, valid coupon to a consumer, the coupon then had the potential to be counterfeited. Expiration dates were tampered with and the mass distribution of the phony coupons could cost a company millions of dollars in losses.

Even the most unassuming citizen could be involved with coupon fraud. On the surface, Connie Arvidson of Boca Raton, Florida, seemed a lot like I was in the 1980s: married, desiring to stay home with her young daughter, and using couponing and refunding to help make ends meet. Only for Arvidson, it didn't stop there. "Coupon Connie" got involved in selling counterfeit coupons for free products. Arvidson was convicted for her part in a nationwide scheme to buy and sell counterfeit coupons worth two million dollars. The mastermind in this scheme was a West Texan, used car salesman in his forties, David Rackmill.

Rackmill was arrested in March 1989 by US Postal Inspector Sam Prose. Rackmill was a convicted con man, an ex-crack addict, and a suspect in a non-related mail fraud case. He consented to a search of his trailer that revealed only a few coupons, but also phone bills with lots of calls to "Coupon Connie." After a weekend in jail, Rackmill was ready to deal. His duplex was searched, where hundreds of thousands of counterfeit coupons were found. Rackmill had used a printer to crank out phony high-value coupons such as $9 off Maxwell House and coupons for free Folgers coffee and Luvs diapers. During the next three months, authorities used Rackmill as bait, taping conversations with his clients, including one of his biggest, "Coupon Connie" Arvidson. Over six months' time, she had allegedly paid him between thirty thousand dollars and forty thousand dollars for coupons worth ten times that amount, reselling them for an estimated eighty thousand dollars in profits. When she was caught, the trunk of her car was loaded with cardboard boxes stuffed with neatly stacked identical free coupons.

In January of 1990, Arvidson was sentenced to federal prison by a Dallas jury. When news stories about her went nationwide, a vague sense of unease reverberated through the coupon clipping community as a whole. For some, the hobby of coupon clipping was abandoned entirely. *"A housewife going to jail for using too many coupons?"* we wondered. *"Could I be next? Am I doing something wrong?"* For the first time in my history of couponing, I wasn't proud to divulge the fact that I was an avid coupon user. I'd cringe at the checkout when I'd hand over my stack of coupons to the cashier, occasionally hearing, "These aren't fake coupons are they, like that woman in Florida?" Extreme couponers throughout the nation experienced a collective shame.

A few years went by and everyone seemed to forget about "Coupon Connie." I breathed a huge sigh of relief, reveling once again in my shopping skills and a local celebrity status as Coupon Queen.

At least I did until 2012, when the popular TLC series, *Extreme Couponing* brought an increased scrutiny of coupons at the checkout, and for good reason. Long-time couponers were up in arms after it was obvious that one of the first participants on the program had used coupons in a way that screamed "coupon misredemption," taking advantage of the family coding of various coupons to use them on products they were not intended for. As if that weren't suspicious enough, future episodes of *Extreme Couponing* featured shoppers who were blatantly using counterfeit coupons. In

October of 2011, one of the shoppers used thirty-four free 12-pack Quilted Northern toilet paper coupons. Those coupons turned out to be counterfeit. The Gelson's store that accepted the coupons discovered this when they were denied payment for them. The teen shopper's mother had to come in and repay the store for over four hundred dollars' worth of toilet paper, but viewers never saw that on television.

Then in a 2012 episode, a Pennsylvania shopper used two hundred coupons for free bottles of Tide. Those coupons also turned out to be fraudulent. Both Jill Cataldo and the CIC were instrumental in bringing these counterfeit coupons to light, and yet the TLC producers had little more to say about the problem than claiming they had no responsibility for the coupons their featured shoppers used. Where did the shoppers get their fake coupons? While not verified, they likely bought them, maybe from someone like Robin Ramirez of Phoenix, Arizona. After an eight-week undercover investigation, in July of 2012, police raided the homes of three Phoenix area women, seizing forty million dollars' worth of very realistic-looking counterfeit coupons. They also seized two million dollars' worth of assets from the three homes. The women allegedly purchased the fake coupons overseas and then resold them through a website, SavvyShopperSite.com, and through auctions on eBay.

When it comes to counterfeiting coupons, the advent of the Internet and Internet-printed (IP) coupons brought its own share of problems. The first IP coupons were a PDF file that could be printed over and over. It took me awhile to trust the IP coupons when they were first introduced. It seemed too good to be true; that I could just print out coupon after coupon with my printer. It soon was. The first wave of counterfeit IP coupons hit stores in Southeast United States in late 2002 through 2003. It got so bad that, by August of 2003, major newspapers were reporting that many grocers had stopped taking the coupons downloaded from the Internet.

The Georgia Food Industry Association reported that the counterfeiting was the biggest coupon scam to hit Georgia in more than fourteen years. The coupons that began as a legitimate offer were reproduced with altered discounts and expiration dates, and were distributed via the Internet. Most were for free items, with altered bar codes realistic enough to fool even the store scanners.

Auction web sites such as Yahoo and eBay were at least partially responsible for the rise in counterfeit coupon use because they allowed auctions of large groups of coupons as well as auction listings of Internet coupons. In an August 2003 letter that was sent to both auction sites, the Grocery Manufacturers of America and the Food Marketing Institute requested the ban of all coupon auctions. While it is difficult to ascertain exact amounts, in the letter the two industry groups cited estimates of between five hundred and eight hundred million dollars in lost revenue from counterfeit coupons. Yahoo responded by banning all sales of coupons in October 2003. On the other hand, eBay only banned auctions of electronic and bulk coupons. By March of 2004, they had also banned bulk sales of more than twenty coupons for one product or one hundred mixed coupons. They limited the sale of "free product" and home-printed Internet coupons to two per listing. An individual was also designated by eBay in its fraud-investigating department to work with packaged-goods representatives to monitor coupon listings. And yet, to this day, with very little effort, I was able to unearth auction listings of "free product" coupons that are questionable, considering the same seller has listed and sold hundreds of similar sets.

For a long time I believed that people like Coupon Connie were an exception to the rule and the major players in coupon fraud were the fake storefronts, coupon brokers, and crooked business-men. Certain that fraud and deception was only prevalent among the big-wigs of the coupon industry, I was blissfully unaware that, in 1983, Postal authorities had begun an investigation of refund conventions, code-named "Rebategate."

8¢

The Refund Racket

For a refunder in the 1980s, the old adage "you can never be too rich or too thin" could easily have included "or have too many qualifiers." Can there ever be too much of a good thing? In an October 1987 *Atlantic Journal and Atlantic Constitution* article about refunds, Dr. Sam Dietz, professor of educational psychology at Georgia State University, was quoted as saying, "Receiving refunds in the mail acts as a positive reinforcement, so refunding may be a compulsive behavior."

As a stay-at-home mom in the late 1980s and early 1990s, I was hooked on free stuff. The only adults I interacted with on a consistent basis were the UPS driver and the postal delivery worker. Boxes of company premiums arrived on my porch at least once a week, and my mailbox was full of samples, free coupons, and advertising T-shirts in sealed plastic bags. Walks with my children included forays into alleys where we collected proofs of purchase from other people's garbage. A trip to the park meant dipping into the trash cans for stray candy bar wrappers. Weekly, and yes, sometimes even daily trips to the recycling center were a form of entertainment my older children grew up with. Who needs nights at the movies or theme parks when there are open recycling bins just ten blocks from home?

When I inherited a previous neighbor's stash of trash, you'd have thought I'd won the lottery. After we carted it all home, I spent hours on my back porch sorting through it all: rubber-banding box tops and box bottoms together, filling a bin with empty M&M candy bags, and taping and paper-clipping small proofs of purchase to blank note cards. That winter I was able to order a dozen strings of M&M Christmas lights and at least as many $5 AT&T gift certificates with my inheritance. Every time I visited my parents, I came home with Folgers' lids and Del Monte labels my mother had saved for me. When Folgers offered a free coffeemaker, I ordered one for her, another for myself, and had yet another sent to my sister's house for her family. When the Gloria Vanderbilt Company offered a lovely feminine umbrella in exchange for an empty box, I didn't have to purchase any perfume since I had two flattened boxes in my file cabinet. The majority of the offers didn't require a receipt, but I saved every one of my receipts and picked others up from the parking lot, just in case. Our small-town grocery store didn't have itemized receipts, so if a refund required a cash register tape, I either used one I had stapled to the empty box or included one from the grocery store with the approximate price.

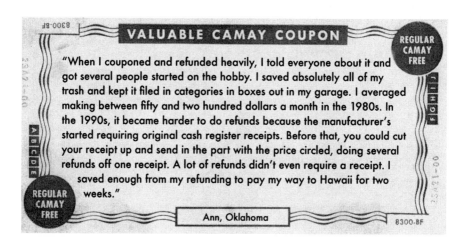

VALUABLE CAMAY COUPON

REGULAR CAMAY FREE

"When I couponed and refunded heavily, I told everyone about it and got several people started on the hobby. I saved absolutely all of my trash and kept it filed in categories in boxes out in my garage. I averaged making between fifty and two hundred dollars a month in the 1980s. In the 1990s, it became harder to do refunds because the manufacturer's started requiring original cash register receipts. Before that, you could cut your receipt up and send in the part with the price circled, doing several refunds off one receipt. A lot of refunds didn't even require a receipt. I saved enough from my refunding to pay my way to Hawaii for two weeks."

Ann, Oklahoma

Compulsive? I lived and breathed refunding, and my children benefited with their wide variety of toys, balls, and T-shirts I obtained through my hobby. It was all a big game, and one that I played well. And I was not alone. While there was no estimate available on the number of people who were involved in refunding, Carol Backs, publisher of *Money Maker* magazine in the late 1980s and chairman of a trade association of refund magazine publishers, claimed that refund magazines were selling eight hundred thousand to one million subscriptions.

Not once during this time did I believe I was doing something morally suspect or illegal by having my mother save labels, digging in recycling centers, or ordering extra coffee-makers with lids from coffee that someone else drank. But if I'd been among those receiving "the letter" from the Postmaster General that I'd heard about in the refund bulletins and magazines, perhaps I would have thought differently. I'd seen vague references to it in my refund magazines and bulletins but didn't think it applied to me. I hadn't traded with any of the women who were indicted for fraud or I would have gotten one, too.

OFFICE OF THE INSPECTOR IN CHARGE
REBATE FRAUD TASK FORCE
Cincinnati, OH 45202-5748

January 30, 1997

3

Dear Postal Customer:

This office is investigating a possible violation of Federal Law involving rebate activity with which you may be associated.

We sometimes find that individuals are unaware that they may be in violation of the Mail Fraud Statutes. Other times we find that individuals intentionally defraud businesses and serious conse-quences are the end result. Our main objective at this point, where a violation exists, is to see that the use of the mail is terminated. Continued activity could result in prosecutive action and the related criminal penalties.

Rebating schemes are illegal under the Mail Fraud Statute, Title 18 Section 1341 and under the False Representation Law, Title 39, Section 3005, United States Code.

Manufacturers offer rebates to individuals to induce the individ-uals to buy their products. These offers are limited to a certain number per household and are limited to the individual who actually purchased the product.

When an individual submits an application for a rebate, the individ-ual is expressly or implicitly representing to the manufacturer that the individual has actually purchased the product (as opposed to an individual who has traded for the proof of purchase with another, or purchased the proof of purchase, or manufactured the proof of purchase or obtained it by some other means). The individual is also represent-ing that he or she is complying with the terms of the rebate offer in respect to the number of rebates requested on this particular product. When an individual uses multiple addresses such as post office boxes or variations of the street address or multiple fictitious names, the individual is falsely representing to the manufacturer that each sub-mitted rebate request is the only rebate requested for his or her house-hold. The individual is also causing something of value, namely the rebate check, to be sent through the mail in furtherance of a scheme to defraud. Likewise, if an individual claims a rebate on a product that the individual did not personally purchase, the individual is also making a misrepresentation, unless a rebate form expressly states that no pur-chase of a product is necessary to obtain a rebate.

- 2 -

Once an individual is put on notice that certain conduct is illegal, that individual could be shown to have the necessary criminal intent for prosecution should the individual continue to engage in that activity.

If after reviewing your activities in light of the applicable statutes, you feel you unknowingly became involved in rebating activity that may be a violation of the law and now wish to disassociate yourself from this activity, please advise us by filling out the enclosed form and returning it. If you choose to disassociate yourself from the activity, you should write "REFUSED" across the face of any mail received by you in connection with the activity, mark a line through your name and address, and return it to the post office for return to sender. However, should you wish to discuss any aspect of this matter please call 1-800-353-8177. If in your opinion you believe this Voluntary Discontinuance notice does not apply to you, please detail in writing your reasons and return them to this office in the enclosed envelope along with a telephone number where you can be reached during the day. Also, please include the control number which appears in the upper right hand portion of the notice. All information you provide will be investigated and verified. Our primary concern is to see fraudulent activity stopped to ensure the integrity of the U. S. Mail.

R. J. Bowdren
Postal Inspector in Charge

Enclosures

In the earlier referenced October 1987 *Atlantic Journal and Atlantic Constitution* article, John Smietanka, a US attorney for the Western district of Michigan referred to refunders as "a subculture with its own jargon, clubs, conventions, and magazines."

Unfortunately, all these offers that were designed to entice consumers to buy specific products by offering incentives like cash, premiums, and free coupons did something else: they enticed people to cheat.

For a group of people so eager to share their stories regarding coupon savings and memorable refund offers, I was surprised at how many clammed up when it came to the subject of refund conventions and refund fraud. One woman who excitedly shared her enthusiasm for the hobby stopped answering my e-mails when I asked about her experiences at refund conventions. She later emailed an apology and confided that she'd actually been convicted of mail fraud, fined, and put on a two years' probation. Her crime? She'd rented several PO boxes to get around the "one per address" rule of refunds.

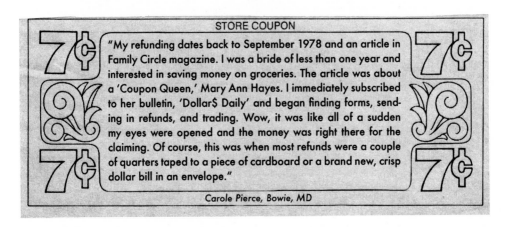

STORE COUPON

"My refunding dates back to September 1978 and an article in Family Circle magazine. I was a bride of less than one year and interested in saving money on groceries. The article was about a 'Coupon Queen,' Mary Ann Hayes. I immediately subscribed to her bulletin, 'Dollar$ Daily' and began finding forms, sending in refunds, and trading. Wow, it was like all of a sudden my eyes were opened and the money was right there for the claiming. Of course, this was when most refunds were a couple of quarters taped to a piece of cardboard or a brand new, crisp dollar bill in an envelope."

Carole Pierce, Bowie, MD

Another woman stated that she'd personally known some of the women who were making thousands of dollars a month with refunds and who brought their cash registers with them to conventions. She minimized her own involvement, stating that she'd only had four or five PO boxes. When I asked more questions, she stopped talking. I didn't want names, only stories, yet so many seemed hesitant to share even those.

Others had no problem sharing their fond memories of those days: the conventions where they never saw or heard of any illegal or suspect activities. Instead, these women enjoyed a room full of couponing comrades, a good lunch, some door prizes, and a frenzy of trading forms and coupons. Evidently, there were two different types of conventions being held: those that included questionable activities and those of a more innocent nature, designed for legitimate trading and fun.

A former refunder from Washington, who wished to remain anonymous, wrote:

A friend and I held a refunding convention in the Washington area during the spring or summer of 1975. Most people who attended were just regular folks who did the allowable number of submissions for each refund. There were a lot more refunds back then. The other types of refunders showed up too. My friend and I saw two people sitting across a table from each other. Each had a tall stack of complete deals in front of them. They were both candid that they used multiple names and addresses and made over 1000 dollars per month each in refunds doing so. Another woman told us that she had her home address set up as an apartment building with twenty-four apartments so that she could do multiples of each refund. We met a woman whose husband worked in an auto shop so she obtained lots of oil and oil-filter UPCs and auto rebate forms. She bought a cash register so she could make her own receipts. On that day she had 300 oil filter complete deals available to sell or trade for. The other "high rollers" present specialized in alcohol deals. They would obtain empty liquor bottles from recycle facilities and make up complete deals creating their own cash register tapes. These "big girls," as we called them, were completely open about the number of offers they submitted.

My friend and I were so shocked by some of these people that we never held another convention, even though there was a big demand for us to do so. Years later, (in the late 1980s to the early 1990s) we attended conventions where

*people came from great distances. We met a woman who
specialized in liquor deals. It turned out she had so many
addresses in multiple states and she made so much money
at it that she actually flew to her various mail drops to
pick up her checks. Very shortly after what became our
last convention, there was a lot of publicity about the
"bust" at a refunding convention in upstate New York.
"Coupon Connie's" infamous arrest for printing fake
coupons happened around that time, too. My friend and I
decided it was not worth it to attend or hold conventions
that essentially became a clearinghouse for some people
to engage in inappropriate and illegal activities related to
refunding. Over the years we became very disillusioned
about what people would do to make a few bucks.*

More long-time couponers and refunders had only good
memories, unaware of anything illegal or morally questionable
going on at the conventions they attended. Betty Burrison was one
of them. She remembered:

*In 1981, I moved to Maryland from New Jersey and
became friends with a gal who refunded and used coupons,
which I was also into. We were close to the Pennsylvania
border and found out about a convention that was to be
held there, so we decided to go. We arrived early with
all our duplicate coupons, proofs of purchase, and extra
refund forms. We signed in, paid a small fee that covered
lunch, sat at one of the tables, and started trading. We
had a ball. There was never any money involved. We had
a great time and met many men and women who enjoyed
our hobby. The women who ran the convention had all*

kinds of door prizes, and the money we paid to attend was used toward the rental of the fire hall where the convention was held. We were able to attend two conventions and came home with lots of forms and coupons to use."

In 1982, postal authorities had begun an investigation code-named "Rebategate" that eventually netted indictments in 1987. The defendants were accused of using false names and addresses and counterfeit cash register tapes to bilk manufacturers out of more than eighty thousand dollars in refunds and rebates. This wasn't the first of such investigations, nor would it be the last. But the fallout wasn't immediately felt by the refund community, at least not until authorities began scrutinizing housewives and church groups.

In 1987, a Michigan couple was indicted on charges of illegally receiving twenty-four thousand dollars from a "$100 rebate" program offered by RJR Nabisco Inc. and RCA Corporation. Some might argue that the company should have foreseen the potential for fraud when they offered such a large sum and only required a sales receipt as proof of purchase for the RCA products. They didn't have the foresight to limit the refund to one per family or address either. Evidently they hadn't even considered the possibility of counterfeit cash register tapes.

Then there was the 1991 operation, dubbed "The Hawkeye Project" after the Hawkeye nickname for the state of Iowa; it was set up by brand manufacturers and the Rebate Information Center, along with investigators from the US Postal Service.

It all seemed harmless enough; families saving their empty boxes, can labels, and receipts and dropping them off at their local fundamentalist Christian school where volunteers would remove the proofs of purchase and attach them to refund forms to send in for cash refunds. "It was like a modern day quilting bee," one resident was quoted as saying in the February 21, 1992, *Wall Street Journal*.

For years, this "Cash for Trash" program was enormously successful, raising an estimated five hundred thousand dollars over two decades. There was only one problem: it was illegal. It wasn't the refunding itself that was illegal, but how it was done: by altering names and addresses for the checks to be mailed to. Most refunds limited the number of redemption offers a household could submit. To get around that clause, residents misspelled their name or changed their address slightly. When addresses of 982 claims were compared with the Postal Service's verified list, 551 of them, or 56 percent, didn't match.

What tipped off the authorities were the suspiciously high rebate rates in the town of Rock Valley, Iowa, with a population of 2540 residents, eleven churches, and the two private religious schools that residents supported with their trash. While the average response rate to a rebate offer from an Iowa zip code was perhaps 5 percent of all households, the town of Rock Valley had mind-boggling 62 percent response rate. At least one resident reported receiving as much as eighty dollars a day using more than two dozen variations of his first and last name.

In this case, authorities concluded that the people involved in raising money for their schools had no intention of breaking the law, so they were simply ordered by the Postal Service to cease and desist the questionable activities.

Another school in the same corner of Iowa doing the same type of fundraising faced a similar inspection from postal authorities, but didn't get into trouble. What was the difference in the two programs? That Iowa school had adhered to the one rebate per family rule, and never altered or duplicated names or addresses to get the refunds.

It wasn't long before refund conventions also became the target of sting operations. In the fall of 1993, a US Postal inspector and state policemen armed with a search warrant walked into a Kanona, New York, refund convention where thirty-one people were about to enjoy lunch. Exactly what were they looking for? They were searching for materials being used for forgery and mail fraud.

Shaken convention attendees were questioned and their refund forms and proofs of purchase confiscated. The postal inspectors had to rent a Ryder truck to remove all the boxes, files, suitcases, and cash registers. Yes, cash registers. Information netted from a computer at the Coupon Information Center in Alexandria, Virginia, had prompted the raid. In 1992, the computer began showing unusual statistics for refund redemption in the Kanona zip code area. The town boasted a staggering 185 times the national average for rejections, equivalent to 767 percent of the deliverable addresses.

THIS COUPON WORTH...10¢

10¢   "I've been doing this since 1978, and boy, how the times have changed. I remember every weekend taking off for a refund convention. The money that was made was unbelievable! I saw hundred dollar bills flying across the beds in hotels where the trading and buying of qualifiers and complete deals were going on. Unreal. Vegas was the mecca for the conventions. If you could afford Vegas, you were in the 'big leagues.' I used to go to Vegas with the gang. I had so many forms I had to put them in a trunk and pay extra at the airport when we were flying. We used to tip the carhops at the casinos with free coupons, I kid you not. The cash registers were another story. It was always a 'keep up with the Joneses' to see who could get the state of the art register and the program to go with it."   **10¢**

Anonymous, convicted of mail fraud, fined, and put on probation

For someone like me who had never attended a refund convention, their subsequent demise was of little consequence. But even the most isolated refunder would hear about Ellen Biles, a Norcross, Georgia, woman indicted for rebate fraud. Biles was arrested at a March 19, 1993, refund convention she was hosting. Authorities began investigating Ms. Biles after a Pep Boys automotive center in Norcross received an anonymous letter accusing Biles of creating false Pep Boys receipts and selling them along with $5 rebate claims on tires. Store managers had received fifty-five claims from across the country for tires supposedly bought at the Norcross store. Most of the receipts were dated October 28, 1992. Evidence submitted at her trial revealed that Biles had received in excess of seven hundred thousand dollars from her fraudulent rebate business between December 1990 and March of 1993. Besides renting out post office boxes under alias names, she taught others how to use her questionable methods to wealth in a monthly bulletin called, "Ellen and Tony's Catalog."

"I remember reading in her bulletin about how to make a Pringles lid work for half a dozen offers instead of a single offer and how to make shampoo hinges that looked genuine for those offers that required only a hinge and a code written from the bottle. And of course, she also published the code or even tracings of parts of the bottles that were required for the refund. I wouldn't even need to purchase the product to get the refunds. It was all about beating the system and getting back as much as possible from the manufacturers," one former subscriber told me.

By the time Dateline NBC picked up the story in a May 1995 report, "The Rebate Game," no one wanted to hold or attend any refund conventions, in case they, too, would be targeted by investigators.

These "professional" refunders did more than tarnish the image of refunding. Their illegal activities prompted manufacturers to require much more than a simple receipt for a refund and led to a sharp decline in the number of refunds offered. By the mid-1990s most of us had abandoned collecting and saving our trash in preparation for the next "big deal." I built a bonfire with my labels in 1998. Refunding had changed forever, but at least I could count on my hobby of couponing to remain the same.

Or could I?

The Evolution of the Coupon

Forget the little old lady holding up the checkout lane, scrambling in the bottom of her purse for a stray coupon. Today, she is just as likely to be reaching for her cellphone for savings. Historically, for over one hundred years, the coupon was a piece of paper, but that has changed rapidly in recent years. The majority of the coupons I used in the 1980s had the statement "No Expiration Date" printed right on them. The earliest coupons certainly didn't contain bar codes at the bottom for register scanners that hadn't yet been invented. The GTIN-12 Universal Price Code that allowed cashiers to automatically scan coupons instead of manually entering them wasn't introduced until 1974. In 2007, GS1 bar codes started appearing on the right, alongside the traditional code. A newer system of coding started replacing all the 12-digit

UPCs at the beginning of 2010, offering more features for both stores and manufacturers to track and monitor sales and customize the coupon savings.

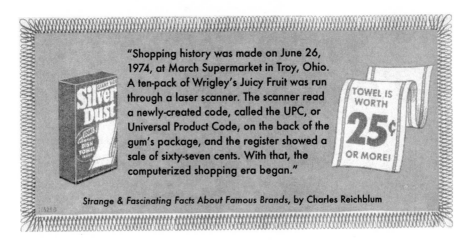

"Shopping history was made on June 26, 1974, at March Supermarket in Troy, Ohio. A ten-pack of Wrigley's Juicy Fruit was run through a laser scanner. The scanner read a newly-created code, called the UPC, or Universal Product Code, on the back of the gum's package, and the register showed a sale of sixty-seven cents. With that, the computerized shopping era began."

Strange & Fascinating Facts About Famous Brands, by Charles Reichblum

Manufacturers were preparing to drop the UPC-A bar code on coupons and use only the GS1 Data Bar by January 2011. However, the transition for retailers who needed to update point of sale software and scanners resulted in a more gradual change with the extended deadline of summer 2011 for a complete elimination of the old code. The new codes included an expiration date, assuring coupons aren't used after the set date. Better yet, the new data bar completely eliminated one of the most flagrant abuses of coupons: that of using a coupon on a related item that it isn't specified for, such as a "$10 tooth-whitening" coupon on a package of diapers made by the same manufacturer.

Never considered the possibility that a consumer would blatantly and routinely do such a thing? I hadn't either, until I unearthed forum archives on the website Dealideal.com that contained incriminating information. Postings dated before 2010 reflected a grave concern over the future update of the barcodes. Apparently, before the anticipated changes, members had been "reading" coupon bar codes so they could figure out which ones would scan for products they weren't designated for. Newbies to the site were advised to use self checkouts or U-scan lanes to avoid getting caught at the practice of deception. Advice on the forum ranged from decoding coupons to redeem on items that weren't listed, to using it on fewer products than what was stated. For example, a coupon good for one dollar off six yogurts might actually scan on the purchase of a single yogurt, netting free yogurt. Members of the forum advocated an awareness of the "family code" in some manufacturer's coupon codes. Certain numbers on the coupon meant it didn't require verification of what it could be redeemed for. In other words, a high-value coupon meant for whitening strips could scan on a package of diaper wipes made by the same company. With these older "family codes," the register accepted the coupon on a variety of products made by the same manufacturer. That system allowed for both unintentional and intentional misredemption. Someone intent on fraudulently using one of those coupons only had to visit the website that offered a "decoder" to find out which other products the coupon worked on.

"Has decoding gone? How long will it take to crack the new code?" asked someone on the Dealideal forum in December of 2008.

The answer?

"The decoding community seems to be in deep denial about this looming catastrophe! Best I can tell from reading the UPC companies' websites, the new system cannot be manipulated because the level of specificity is very high (i.e. dates, quantities, and specific items/combinations). This means that when stores do fully switch over to the new system (i.e. program their terminals to ignore the older, decodable UPC design starting on 1/1/2010), then no "creative" coupon use will be possible! Our only hope thereafter is that stores will continue to read either set for at least a while but eventually even that hope will be gone. So get ready to stockpile like it's 2099!"

Creative couponing? That's one way to put it, but it still boils down to misredemption of a coupon when a consumer is purposely using a coupon on something the coupon wasn't intended for. And when Bud Miller of the Coupon Information Center (CIC) posted informative links regarding counterfeit coupons, forum members booed and hissed in response. "Who let the coupon troll in here?" one poster asked.

Unfortunately for the coupon community, until the codes were changed to eliminate the possibility of using a family code coupon on something it isn't meant for, there would be repeat offenders who aimed to beat the system, fraudulently or not. As recently as April 2011, a couponer featured on the TLC *Extreme Couponing* show admitted to having done just that, right on national television. Legitimate couponers emailed the station, blogged about the controversy, and even created a Facebook page designed specifically for the purpose of jailing this woman for her blatant misuse of coupons. Careful perusal of her filmed purchases and a close-up of her shopping list showed she was shopping by the UPC codes, and not the product name. Versions of her earlier YouTube videos demonstrated how she routinely used coupons for products other than what they were intended for. With the potential for coupon misuse such as this, it is no wonder the manufacturers saw a need to overhaul the Universal Price Codes.

An overhaul of the price codes is just the tip of the iceberg regarding updates and changes in coupons. With the advent of the Internet in the 1990s, a whole new world opened up for coupons. Consumer Product Goods (CPG) marketers budgeted an increasing amount of their advertising dollars towards online marketing. Thrifty Americans began trading in their scissors for downloadable printable coupons and online coupon codes.

The Internet is a logical place to deliver coupons to a web savvy culture. After all, everybody and their grandmother is on the web. For someone who had to be dragged, kicking and screaming, to sign up for a Facebook account, I now log on several times a day. The initial attraction wasn't that I could connect with family and friends—though that was an added bonus—the real attraction was the coupons.

"If you 'Like' Frito-Lay, you can download a $1 coupon on Facebook," someone would post on RefundCents.com, and a host of others would concur.

"Like" Frito-Lay? Download a coupon? I didn't even know what that meant. As a serious technophobe, I dug in my heels and resisted for months, despite the fact that my writing magazines reiterated the importance of authors joining the social network. I finally caved, joining Facebook in August of 2008 when the message boards were buzzing about particularly enticing coupons for as high as eight dollars or even sixteen dollars, coupons only available for users of Facebook. I was skeptical, but ready to join in the fun.

Only that fun turned out to be fraudulent.

Vyrl Market, Inc. had been running a test to find out how people would react to coupons shared among friends in a social community. They planted fifteen different coupons for items such as yogurt, vitamins, and snacks on a new commercial application on Facebook. The hope was that Facebook users would see the coupons and start passing them along to friends. The majority of the images used were downloaded from the Internet, most without the permission of the manufacturers. As the test was getting underway, the coupons were copied and manipulated for different amounts by computer hackers, then posted for people to download. Even my introduction to Facebook was marred

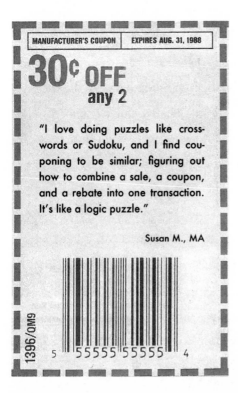

MANUFACTURER'S COUPON | EXPIRES AUG. 31, 1988

30¢ OFF
any 2

"I love doing puzzles like crosswords or Sudoku, and I find couponing to be similar; figuring out how to combine a sale, a coupon, and a rebate into one transaction. It's like a logic puzzle."

Susan M., MA

1396/0M9

5 55555 55555 4

by coupon fraud. Fortunately, I hadn't downloaded any of the coupons, thinking it had sounded too good to be true. Which, of course, it was.

Retailers were learning about the new world of coupons right along with the consumer. When Target initially began issuing their own store-printable coupons that could be combined with manufacturer's coupons, they didn't limit the amount of coupons customers could print out and redeem. People like me took advantage of that, printing out ten to twenty coupons on body wash, and then gathering manufacturer coupons for the same brand. Combined, the two coupons netted bottles of body wash for less than a dime. That year I gave baskets of body wash to all my siblings, completing the gift with a one-dollar body puff. Voila! Cheap gift! It wasn't long before Target began limiting the number of their coupons that could be used each transaction, ruining a bit of the fun for extreme couponers. Cashing in on two cheap body washes isn't nearly as exciting as getting ten bottles for a dollar.

The web, by its very nature of reaching millions of people and defying regulation, also made counterfeiting coupons easier than ever. The very first Internet coupons were PDF files that could easily be copied or manipulated with a different value amount or expiration date. Just as consumer product makers embraced the ease of the Internet for coupon distribution, the first wave of counterfeit Internet-printed coupons hit the stores in 2002. By 2003 stores across the country were refusing to accept any coupons printed from the Internet.

Purveyors of printable coupons such as SmartSource, CoolSavings, and Coupons.com got savvy fairly quickly, coding the coupons to track them and developing a program that only allowed two printings per computer of each coupon. With some of those safeguards in place, stores that had initially banned Internet coupons started accepting them again.

According to the Carolina Manufacturer Services Incorporated, by 2001, consumers were downloading 114 million coupons, and by the first half of 2010, NCH Marketing Services reported that the Internet was the fastest growing way of distributing coupons. Reports from Google Insights in mid-2010 showed that Internet searches for "printable coupons" increased 67 percent over a year before, for the first time surpassing searches for "Britney Spears."

Data released by Coupons.com in February 2010 showed an increase in printed savings of over 170 percent during 2009. They reported a staggering one billion dollars in savings printed from the Coupons.com network in 2009, and a 220 percent increase in coupon printings from 2008 to 2009. According to an Inmar study, businesses issued 367 billion coupons in 2009, and buyers redeemed 3.3 billion. Online coupon access, however, increased by 92 percent, and redemption of Internet deals leaped by 360 percent. Cereal has remained the most popular category for coupon use, followed by yogurt, snacks, and pizza. Top advancing categories included restaurants and entertainment.

Will we someday see a completely paperless couponing universe? Electronic coupons, arriving by cellphone, Twitter, email, and Facebook are bringing in the new, younger customers, those who have previously rejected the paper coupon. As of February 2010, more than forty-five million American consumers are now using online coupons, representing over 20 percent of the US population. Of those, almost one third (13.1 million) do not clip coupons from their Sunday paper. The consumer who prints digital coupons has an average household income of $97,000, and is even more likely to have a college degree than those who use newspaper coupons.

The number of consumers using their mobile phone for coupons is increasing exponentially as well. According to a Juniper Research November 2009 report, over fifty million consumers already use their mobile devices for coupons, and they estimate that as many as 200 million mobile subscribers will be redeeming them by 2013. Many coupons are now entirely electronic— uploaded to a store's loyalty card or arriving on a cell phone as a promotion code. Store loyalty cards are registered with Coupons. com (a leader in digital couponing) or other similar networks where users can browse available coupons and select the offers they want saved to their card. When the card is scanned at the checkout, the coupons are automatically deducted. The transition linking digital promotions to loyalty cards wasn't much of a stretch; shoppers had already developed a habit of swiping their store card for discounts.

The new frugal are a tech-savvy bunch. Consumers are increasingly turning to their phones for tasks such as comparing prices as well as using applications that allow them to download a coupon. With "Smartphones" like the iPhone and Blackberry, coupon apps are the new wave of the future. An August 2012 report from CouponCabin.com showed that nearly one in five smartphone owners who use coupons say they have an app on the device that is specifically designed for coupons. That number was even higher for men ages eighteen to thirty-four, with 30 percent saying they had a coupon app on their phone. In a recent report, Juniper research found that the total redemption value of mobile coupons will exceed forty-three billion dollars globally by 2016. One such program, SavingStar, is an electronic service and mobile app. It was launched in April 2011, and can be used at over 110 chains in fifty states, including drugstores like CVS and Rite Aid. Discounts are not given at the checkout, but instead "banked" in an account that can be cashed out or transferred to a bank account.

With digital coupons, the redemption rate can be as high as 15 to 20 percent, versus the 1 percent redemption rate of paper coupons, so what's to stop mobile coupons from completely replacing paper?

Me, or people like me.

Keep in mind my initial resistance to joining Facebook. The same technophobia that made me resist signing up for Facebook has prevented me from purchasing and using a Smartphone. Then there is also the high price of the phone itself. Perhaps one of the reasons that more digital coupon users have higher incomes is because they can afford the computers, printers, and Smartphones. We also need to consider the "user apathy" mentioned in a Juniper Research November 2009 report on mobile coupons,

"Mobile Coupons & NFC Smart Posters: Strategies, Applications & Forecasts 2009–2014." The report found that user apathy and a lack of willingness to change and learn new technology are potential road blocks in the mobile industry. John Q. Public (or Mary P. Kenyon) just might not be willing to learn a new method of making financial transactions. Sure, I'm now comfortable downloading and printing out a coupon, but I have just as many friends in my age group who have never downloaded a coupon as those that have. And remember, the coupon programs are not without their own kinks. Sometimes the application doesn't work, and I have to update the program in order to use it. Unless I lose my scissors, I don't have a similar problem with my paper coupons. When I go to the store with a fully-stocked coupon box, I can just shuffle through the organized categories to locate a coupon for something I find on the clearance shelf. I can't do that with coupons downloaded on a phone or loaded onto a loyalty card.

These are the kind of problems UA PetSmart associate professor Anita Bhappu discovered when she studied digital coupons. The division chair of retailing and consumer sciences headed up a research project in 2010 that focused on grocery retailing with the use of digital coupons. Bhappu and her student researchers discovered that participants often found the coupons difficult to use. The team held focus groups and administered surveys before and after a one-week trial of digital coupons. The focus groups included heavy users of paper coupons, those Bhappu described as the "coupon divas," as well as non-users of paper coupons. The biggest complaint? After loading digital coupons onto loyalty cards, many could not remember which coupons were available to them.

Being able to see the saved coupons or have them show up automatically in a phone's grocery list application might make a difference in the ease of use. That is now a possibility. Applications like GroceryIQ and GroceryPal already make using digital coupons easier. The future holds even more possibility with a mobile technology company like PointInside that is developing and testing technology that will identify where a shopper is standing in a grocery store and offer that customer coupons based upon where they are and the products that are nearby. In other words, a future scenario might be a coupon program that will virtually nudge the consumer, urging them to purchase a particular product and offering them an incentive. (If you ask me, that sounds too much like taking a couple of kids along when you go shopping, trading in the "Give me, give me," for an equally annoying, "Pick me, Pick me.")

But what about the couponer's compulsion to buy more than one item to take advantage of coupon savings? Stockpiling is the extreme couponer's middle name. Any interest I may have had in mobile coupons promptly disappeared as soon as I realized downloaded coupons would be applied to the purchase of a single product. A one-dollar discount on one item isn't nearly as appealing as clipping ten one-dollar coupons for ten discounted products. Extreme couponers like filling their carts with cheap and free merchandise. Just ask the Kmart Corporation.

When Kmart initially introduced an "up to $2 double coupon event" at select stores nationwide in 2007 and 2008, they limited it to a total of seventy-five coupons and four like items per customer. By shopping with my husband and filling two carts, I'd come home with a total of 150 items for less than twenty dollars. Later, they limited it to twenty-five items per person and my husband and I would go out for lunch after our first coupon spree, and then return that same day for another trip through the checkout. More recently, they were limiting it to five coupons per day with your store card. For that miniscule savings, I don't even bother making the trip.

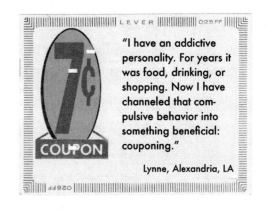

"I have an addictive personality. For years it was food, drinking, or shopping. Now I have channeled that compulsive behavior into something beneficial: couponing."

Lynne, Alexandria, LA

Downloaded coupon savings on a single item is hardly going to appeal to the extreme couponer, but it might prompt someone who has never bothered to clip a paper coupon to take advantage of the savings. Just as with any new technology, there has been a transition period as shoppers and retailers become more comfortable with digital promotions. Some industry experts are skeptical that consumers will download iPhone apps for all the brands they purchase, but they have proven to appeal to a tech-savvy generation that was not tempted to use paper coupons.

Technology also plays a vital role in the lives of today's mothers, and since they reportedly control a whopping 80 percent of all household spending, marketers have had to take note of the time they spend on the Internet. Time on the Internet is the one activity that actually increases after a woman has a baby, maybe because they are searching for the same type of support system I used to find through my homemaking and pen-pal magazines. According to BSM Media, over 75 percent of moms are on Facebook and 76 percent are "fans" of at least one company. Moms rely heavily on the Internet to learn about the products they need and connect with other moms to exchange opinions about retailers and products.

And to save money, of course.

The brands that have been most successful using social media to attract consumers are those that offer coupons and discounts. One fourth of respondents to a survey conducted by Chadwick Martin Bailey said that coupons and discounts were the primary reason they became fans of a brand on Facebook.

It isn't just moms jumping on the Internet bandwagon either. The research group eMarketer estimated that in 2009 users in the forty-five to sixty-three age group made up 28.8 percent of the total online population, to the tune of 57.4 million consumers. While individuals over sixty-five still make up less than 10 percent of the active Internet universe, their numbers are also on the rise.

The Social Networks of Facebook and Twitter have become an attractive venue for retailers to influence consumers. Successful retailers today know the importance of responding to their customers, and what better way than to go where consumers are in the online communities. In April 2011, Facebook joined the coupon market, offering users in five US cities coupons for everything from wine tastings to concert tickets. The special "Deals" coupons were offered directly through the Facebook service at a limited discount price. A week before that, Google Inc. had begun marketing a daily deal service dubbed "Offers" to users in Portland, Oregon.

With these new services, Facebook and Google jumped on the bandwagon of the concept of "daily deals" that was pioneered by Groupon. Somewhat like an online version of the coupons you get in the mail from a local merchant or a Yellow Page ad, Groupon took the coupon discount and added a novelty of requiring a certain amount of consumers to purchase the discount within a set time frame, before it became valid. Christopher Steiner, in an August 2010 *Forbes* article, described it as "a cents-off coupon married to a Friday-after-Thanksgiving shopping frenzy." Groupon's founder, Andrew Mason, came up with the idea while trying to cancel a cell phone contract in 2006. He launched his website, The Point, in 2007 and based it on the "tipping point" principle that would utilize social media to organize collective action. The Point faced mounting losses until Mason noted that one of the website's most effective campaigns was when consumers banded together to gain buying power. He started a blog that offered readers a different deal from various vendors every day. Groupon, then called Getyourgroupon.com, was born.

The growth of Groupon was swift, from about four hundred subscribers when they started in November 2008, to over five million in the United States by mid-2010. Except for YouTube, which reached a value of one billion dollars in twelve months, no other Internet company has grown quite as fast, not even eBay, Amazon, or Google. Less than two years after its inception, Groupon boasted a value of one billion dollars. And unlike

YouTube, founded in 2005 and yet to turn a profit, Groupon was making a profit just seven months after its inception. In fact, Groupon made waves in the business world in early 2011 by turning down a reported six billion–dollar buyout from Google.

This is the concept behind the Groupon service: They find a merchant willing to offer a significant discount on a service or product if a certain amount of people sign up. Groupon advertises and spreads the word of the offer to its members and gets a percentage of the revenue the merchant brings in. On average, the merchant ends up collecting only about 25 percent of what they would normally make, yet the program works as a new and different form of advertising promotion.

Sometimes, it can work too well. In March of 2010, East Coast Aero Club, a flight school in Bedford, Massachusetts, offered introductory helicopter flying lessons, normally priced at $225, for only $69. The deal had to be shut down at 11:00 a.m., after 2,500 subscribers signed up. The club had expected maybe two *hundred* customers.

More than two hundred Groupon copycat sites have sprung up in the United States, with sites like Living Social.com becoming its closest rival. Launching in July 2009, LivingSocial has been giving Groupon a run for their money ever since Amazon jumped on board in December of 2010 with an investment of 175 million dollars. A January 19, 2011, offer of a $20 Amazon gift card for ten dollars didn't hurt either, netting over 1.3 million sales in twenty-four hours, with a total take of over thirteen million dollars in gross sales. In comparison, Groupon's August 2010 offer of a $50

Gap card for $25 reportedly sold 441,000 coupons and generated eleven million dollars in sales. The premise of these sites is the same: Share the deals, and in some cases increase the savings in proportion to the additional number of people taking advantage of the deals. An incentive for sharing the deals might be as enticing as a five- or ten-dollar credit when a friend joins through a referral link. In the future, websites such as Groupon and LivingSocial will likely offer a more personalized service. Groupon's founder, Andrew Mason is already developing what he calls Groupon 2.0, a second phase of social commerce, a hyper-local connection of knowing where subscribers live and what their interests are so they can deliver personalized offers to customer's inboxes.

Whatever their flaws, coupons and online sites will most likely thrive and become even more personalized and accessible. That might be seen as beneficial for the frugal consumer, but the advantages of online coupons are actually greater for the companies themselves. For years, shoppers have been taking advantage of coupons, but now coupons could be taking advantage of the consumer. Some of the new coupons, downloaded from the Internet or sent to mobile phones, are loaded with information about the customer who uses it. The bar codes include information about the customer, their Internet address, and even their Facebook page information. In many cases, the coupons can be traced to the person who printed them.

In a 2010 investigative series, "What They Know," *The Wall Street Journal* looked at just how fundamental web technologies can now jeopardize user privacy, with websites installing new and intrusive consumer-tracking techniques. The Journal's study shows the extent to which web users are exchanging their personal data for access to information and services. They examined the fifty most popular websites in the US to measure the quantity and capabilities of the "cookies" and other trackers installed on a visitor's computer by each site. The fifty sites installed a total of 3,180 tracking files on a test computer used to conduct the study. Only one site, Wikipedia.org, had none installed. Two-thirds of the tracking tools came from 131 companies that are mostly in the business of following Internet users to create databases of consumer profiles that can be sold. The companies that placed the most tools were Google Inc., Microsoft, and Quantcast Corp, all in the business of targeting ads at people online.

Some of the tracking files identified by the Journal were so detailed that they verged on being anonymous in name only. They enabled data-gathering companies to build personal profiles that included age, gender, race, zip code, income, marital status, and health concerns, along with recent purchases and favorite television shows and movies. In some cases a retailer could know that Mary Kenyon printed off a "20% off" coupon after searching for clothing discounts at Ebates.com on Monday morning and redeemed it later that afternoon at the store.

When someone joins a fan club on Facebook, their Facebook ID becomes visible to the merchandiser. When the consumer redeems the offer in the store, the coupon can be tracked back to the Facebook user. A company called RevTrax handles tracking for a large and varied group of companies. Joanathan Treiber,

VALUABLE CAMAY COUPON

YOUR DEALER WILL GIVE YOU

FREE

Results of the 2012 RedPlum "Purse String Study":

- 79% of respondents using mobile coupons are saving up to $50 a week
- 82% of respondents who are using more online coupons are saving up to $50 a week
- 88% of deal seekers are most likely to visit their favorite savings or deal websites at least weekly

REGULAR CAMAY FREE

REGULAR CAMAY FREE

8300-BF

RevTrax's co-founder was quoted in an April 20, 2010 *New York Times* article as saying, "Over time, we'll be able to do much better profiling around certain IP addresses, to say, hey, this IP address is showing a proclivity for printed clothing apparel coupons and is really only responding to coupons greater than 20% off."

The idea of personalized coupon offerings isn't just on the web, either. Brand marketers are learning to become increasingly personal in their coupon offerings, with digital and mobile coupons relevant to today's consumer. In a 2012 *AdWeek* shopper marketing report, it was reported that a "Safeway Just 4 U" program was operating in over 1600 stores in the United States and Canada. The program offers digital coupons based on purchasing histories of the Shopper's Club card. Another grocery store, Kroger, has done the same thing for several years, through a partnership with an analytics company, dunnhumby, offering personalized deals that load directly to the customer's frequent shopper card.

"Brands and retailers are definitely able to better target their campaigns as a result of the amount of data that is at their fingertips today," Marco Muzzi, marketing director at Acuity Ads, said in the *AdWeek* article.

A disturbing thought? Or exactly what we all desire, a personalized savings? After all, everybody loves a good deal. And everyone loves coupons.

Don't they?

Does Couponing Always Make Cents?

The Procter & Gamble company hates me.

Alright, I'll concede they might not hate me, personally, but their intention in dispersing coupons for their products is not to ensure that consumers like me can regularly fill their shopping carts with free merchandise.

In 1996, around the time Procter & Gamble conducted their "zero-coupon" experiment in upstate New York, the *Supermarket News* quoted their president and chief operating officer Durk Jager, as saying "We decided coupons have to go," in regards to the inefficiency of couponing as a promotional tool.

"They encourage switching/promiscuity, and thus over time can reduce brand loyalty," he elaborated in an e-mail to *Ad Age* magazine. "They commoditize categories, since the value of the deal gets greater prominence than the brand itself. They irritate non-coupon users."

Executives at Procter & Gamble have long held this kind of love-hate relationship with coupons. Still, it wasn't until October 2010 that I noticed changes in the Procter & Gamble newspaper coupon insert that suggested their ire was definitely targeted at extreme couponers. For the first time in my long history of using coupons, I saw a qualifier added to the use of a brand's coupons. The newest Procter & Gamble coupons had additional wording in small print at the bottom: "*Limit of four like coupons in same shopping trip. Coupons not authorized if purchasing products for resale.*" Did this mean I could expect the Procter & Gamble coupon police to raid my next garage sale if I included some extra stockpiled items?

Despite a renewed interest in coupon use that corresponded with the downturn in the economy, there are still many packaged-goods marketers and retailers who would like to see paper coupons go the way of the dinosaur, viewing them as annoying or wasteful. And they do have a valid concern. Dealing with the distribution and redemption of coupons has typically been a complicated, costly, and inefficient process.

Even today, coupon processing includes hand counting or gross weighting millions of pieces of paper of varying sizes, often by agents that ship the coupons to clearinghouses in Mexico, where workers sort and scan for hours each day. For those workers, coupons might mean a job, but it is a job that is a literal pain in the neck while they stand in an assembly line, hand sorting and scanning upwards of ten thousand coupons a day. Coupons are counted at least twice, sometimes three times, by various parties. Then there are the time-consuming and expensive discrepancies, adjustments and negotiations among supermarkets, manufacturers, and the redemption agents.

Despite their inherent messiness, consumers aren't about to give up on a mode of savings that is so much under their control. After all, the price savings from a coupon is guaranteed to go directly to the consumer using it. A coupon can allow a consumer to purchase brand-name products at the same, or sometimes even a lower price, than a store brand. And only the coupon-using consumer obtains those benefits. In fact, there are detractors who insist that the coupon user reaps a benefit that serves to increase the prices across the board. Former Grocery Marketing magazine associate publisher Ryan Mathews, was quoted in the November 8, 1992, *Los Angeles Times* as saying couponing is a "Stone Age industry in a high-tech world, one in which manufacturers have run amok by flooding consumers with tons of worthless paper." He asserted that in order to pay for the coupons, product makers merely raise prices, helping a select number of people at the expense of the majority. "No company believes that a fraction of these coupons will be redeemed. In fact, if people redeemed even half of the coupons there wouldn't be enough money in the Treasury to pay for it. The economy would collapse."

As far back as the late 1970s, Presidential Advisor of Consumer Affairs Esther Peterson had criticized coupons as a cost-increasing form of promotion. Her former employer, Giant Foods of

Washington, DC, even produced a film in 1979 that was critical of food coupons. Not surprising, Peterson's criticism was not taken kindly by proponents of coupons and staunch members of coupon clubs.

There is also the camp of coupon detractors who insist that clipping coupons is a complete waste of a consumer's time. In the Summer 1982 issue of the *Journal of Consumer Affairs*, J. N. Uhl, Associate Professor of Agricultural Economics at Purdue University, attempted to prove this point. He insisted the savings to be had with coupons was an illusion. "While some consumers can possibly save money at the expense of higher food prices and other consumers through the use of coupons, it is unlikely that coupons provide any net saving to consumers as a class," he said, and then went on to state, "Since coupon usage does not require talent and has no productive value to the economy, the time and energy costs of coupon savings are a deadweight economic loss. Consumers are being 'paid' to perform tasks which merely redistribute income without producing anything of value. In the coupon game, consumers seem to be donating their time and energy costs in service to the coupon sponsors. Presumably, consumers have better, more productive uses of their time and talents."

No talent? No productive value? Thousands of extreme couponers would disagree. Aren't they the smartest of all shoppers? In fact, some of us are practically geniuses in the art of coupon savings. When a couponer walks out the door of a store with a cartload of free merchandise, they experience what many describe as a natural "high." But according to detractors like Esther Peterson and J. N. Uhl, not only are couponers delusional, but their hobby is increasing prices and a complete waste of our time.

Jane Kolondinsky, an avid couponer and a Professor of the Department of Community Development and Applied Economics at the University of Vermont, studied whether or not the use of coupons was a worthwhile practice for consumers in terms of cost-effectiveness. Published in the *Journal of Consumer Studies and Home Economics* in 1992, she found that a full 40 percent of coupon clippers were not using coupons in a cost-effective manner. That percentage of coupon users studied did not reap savings at least equal to the time cost of their coupon clipping. She then expanded the basic cost-benefit model of coupon use to see if the enjoyment of clipping them was significantly greater for those consumers who were inefficiently using them, but didn't find that to be the case.

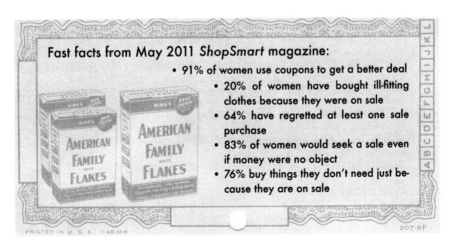

Fast facts from May 2011 *ShopSmart* magazine:
- 91% of women use coupons to get a better deal
- 20% of women have bought ill-fitting clothes because they were on sale
- 64% have regretted at least one sale purchase
- 83% of women would seek a sale even if money were no object
- 76% buy things they don't need just because they are on sale

Maybe it isn't the clipping, the comparing prices, or even the savings itself that gives extreme couponers the "high" they get with their super shopping trips. Perhaps it has more to do with the customer being solely responsible for obtaining the discount, a sort of "smart-shopper" syndrome.

Robert M. Shindler looked at just this possibility in two studies that were published in the *Journal of Consumer Psychology* in 1998. In looking at "coupon queens," for example, he suggested that the anecdotal evidence of price promotions was capable of generating enthusiasm beyond the economic value of the money saved. He measured a consumer's perception of themselves as general "smart shoppers" in regards to their level of involvement in obtaining the discounts. Two possible sources of pride-like feelings in relation to a discount were apparent.

First, there was the *added-weight* explanation: the pride of obtaining a discount might increase the value of the discount by adding weight or importance to the good feelings that accrue from the economic aspect of the discount.

The second possibility was a *joy-of-winning* explanation: perceiving oneself as responsible for a gain of any perceptible size in an implied game against the seller, or even against other consumers.

Could he be right? After some of my super coupon shopping sprees, my daughter Elizabeth, the cradle-couponer mentioned in chapter one, didn't hesitate to point out that in my many trips to a larger town, I am actually spending money, not saving it. A friend once said the same thing.

"You could have saved yourself more than (*whatever amount of money I spent that day*) just by staying home and not buying all those shampoos, deodorants, and air fresheners."

Technically, they are correct. Instead of planning two or three out-of-town shopping trips each month to combine sale prices with coupons, I could have saved the gas money and simply picked up a pack of toilet paper or bottle of shampoo whenever I needed it. But then, the Christmas baskets I fill every year would be out of my price range, I'd have no extra stockpile to share as prizes at my workshops, and my cupboards would be as bare as the proverbial Mrs. Hubbard. That is exactly the way much of America lives and spends, but it doesn't sound like much fun to me.

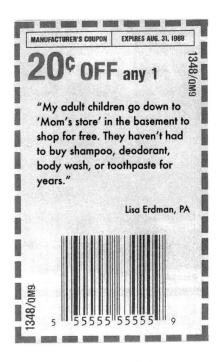

MANUFACTURER'S COUPON — EXPIRES AUG. 31, 1988

20¢ OFF any 1

1348/QM9

"My adult children go down to 'Mom's store' in the basement to shop for free. They haven't had to buy shampoo, deodorant, body wash, or toothpaste for years."

Lisa Erdman, PA

1348/QM9

5 55555 55555 9

But why do I have the tendency to look at the money I "saved" with a coupon, instead of the money I spent? I am guilty of this every time I go to a Walgreens store and purchase items that are on sale with a register rewards promotion. If I buy a Gillette Fusion razor priced at $9.99 and use a $4 coupon, and that razor purchase triggers a $4 register reward good towards my next purchase, I have often told my husband I got the razor for a mere $1.99. What I actually *paid* was $5.99. I tend to take into account the register reward before I even use it, applying it in my mind to the present purchase. I do the same with rebates. When Staples offers a $4.00 rebate on a ream of paper that costs $5.99, I view it as having paid $1.99 for the paper, even before I send for the rebate. Why the skewed math in my mind?

Dan Ariely, Professor at Duke University, behavioral economist and author of *Predictably Irrational*, explains this phenomenon of looking at the money saved instead of the money spent in this way:

> *We play a game of funny math with rebates or register rewards. If you buy a $10 item that comes with a $4 register reward, in your mind you paid only $6, even if you forget to use the register reward. You are pleased with yourself because you account for the money you saved, not for the money you spent.*

There are stores that consistently use this mind-game to their advantage, training their employees to circle the amount the customer has saved on the bottom of the receipt. "You've saved $56," the cashier informed me after one transaction in which I'd bought a vacuum cleaner on sale. What I'd actually done was spend eighty-nine dollars on a vacuum that retailed for ninety dollars everywhere else. I chose the store and the sale simply for the ten-dollar reward I would need to remember to use the following week.

Would it make sense, then, for companies to simply stop offering coupons and just replace them with lower prices? We've already seen how that worked out with Procter & Gamble's zero coupon test and the ready-to-eat cereal manufacturer's reduction in coupons in the 1990s. A coupon is actually less risky to the merchant than straight reductions in price because someone has to physically go to the work of cutting out the coupon and bringing it into the store, and not every customer will do that, only the more price-sensitive customers will. In this respect, coupons offer that type of customer a different price option.

John H. Antil, an Assistant Professor of the Department of Business at the University of Delaware, also took a look at couponing as a promotional tool in an article published in a 1985 *Journal of Consumer Affairs*. He asserted that lowering prices instead of offering coupons would not work. His research pointed out that General Mills had estimated couponing costs are only 3% of the total dollars invested in promotion and that if cereal prices were reduced by the amount a coupon program costs, the price of a box of cereal would decrease by about two-thirds of a cent, hardly the bargain sale we couponers would be looking for to replace our coupon savings. He pointed out that couponing could actually be used to increase the effectiveness of other forms of communications and promotions, and could influence consumers to purchase new products.

Critics of coupons today sound a lot like the foes of trading stamps in the 1950s. An October 1957 *New York Times* article labeled trading stamps both a boon and a bane to retail merchants. Safeway chain called the trading stamp industry "a shell game to distract the consumer from the fact that she is paying higher prices," citing research done by the University of New Mexico Bureau of Business Research that discovered most stores had to raise prices about 4 percent to cover the costs of a stamp plan.

A 1964 study done by two University of Agricultural Economics professors concurred. After studying the matter for almost a year, they concluded that trading stamps added to the cost of a grocery bill to the tune of a whopping (back then) 67 cents a week for the average family.

Grand Union President Lansing had a simple explanation for the popularity of trading stamps in a 1955 *Time* magazine report. "Getting something for nothing and the squirrel instinct—some people even save string." Yep, that pretty much sums up the whole appeal of both trading stamps and coupons—"Some people even save string."

Even as far back as 1916, the United States Supreme Court saw a danger to trading stamps, calling them "an appeal to stupidity." They gave states the authority to make them illegal. They could, but would they dare to? Housewives of the era seemed to be in solid agreement: they loved the trading stamp programs. In a Stanford Research Institute study of the Denver area in the early 1950s, almost two out of three shoppers believed that stamps meant they were getting something for nothing. Customers reported an "inner satisfaction" from using stamps and a "feeling of thriftiness" from redeeming the completed books. Hmm, those comments sound vaguely familiar.

By 1963, figures from a poll conducted by Benson & Benson, Inc. showed that 84 percent of households were saving stamps. Just as with coupons today, statistics showed that it was those from the middle and higher income brackets and the better educated who were the most likely to save trading stamps.

Trading stamps have gone the way of the dinosaur for the most part, with their large-scale demise during the 1970s gas shortages. Will coupons do the same? Are those of us who avidly use coupons wasting our time? Is extreme couponing nothing more than an obsession with getting something free?

Are extreme couponers crazy? Or, crazy like a fox? Let's look at the foibles and lifestyles of some of the extreme couponers, and you can decide for yourself.

Coupon Queens and Coupon Kings

JILL

Jill Cataldo may be a relative newcomer to the world of extreme couponers. She has only been couponing "seriously" since 2005. Before that, she had been one of the average coupon users who would occasionally clip coupons, using only a few a week. It was when she was pregnant with her third child that she began utilizing the Internet to track store sales. It wasn't long before she figured out that the stores ran sales in cycles and that it was wise to follow those cycles and combine the sale prices with coupons to stockpile. When she discovered that manufacturer's coupons could be combined with a store's coupons, she learned to save even more. Between her stockpiling and couponing, she figures she saves at least 70 percent a week on her family's grocery bill. Moreover, she believes anyone can do what she does, and she holds workshops teaching consumers how to do exactly that.

In June of 2008, the *Chicago Sun Times* asked readers for tips on how to save money on groceries. Jill sent in an e-mail explaining her method of saving money, and the newspaper did a feature article on her.

And the rest, as they say, is history. That single newspaper article spawned six follow-up pieces in the *Sun Times*, appearances on numerous Chicago radio stations, and a recurring segment on the Jonathon Brandmeier radio show in Chicago, along with television news features including ABCs *Nightline*, the CBS *Early Show*, and *Fox News*, among others.

With that kind of news coverage, Jill Cataldo had no difficulty attracting potential students for the coupon classes she began conducting in August 2008, and soon her SuperCouponing Workshops went viral (now available via satellite and on DVD). Besides continuing her workshops, Jill writes a nationally-syndicated newspaper column entitled "Super-Couponing Tips," read by over twenty million people each week, and is a popular Chicago radio personality with her savings segment, "Deals of the Week." In other words, Jill has made a career out of couponing.

Jill has also been a voice of reason in the backlash against couponing brought about by the popularity of the "Extreme Couponing" show, and a crusader for integrity and ethics in couponing.

LISA

Lisa Erdman, an avid couponer in Pennsylvania, on the other hand, has been doing the coupon gig for as long as she has been married, nearly thirty-five years. She credits her Aunt "Honey" for getting her started when she and her husband John were first married. They didn't have a lot of money, so when Aunt Honey shared a Duncan Hines cake "$1 refund" form with Lisa, along with a copy of a refund magazine, it piqued her interest. Who didn't want free cake mix? Raising seven children in the coupon-friendly area of Pennsylvania, Lisa credits coupons for her ability to save as much as 90 percent on her grocery bill, depending on the sales, and the double (or even triple at one time) coupon opportunities.

Once her children were all out of the house, Lisa discovered she had an unusual problem—she couldn't stop "buying" all the free stuff local stores were offering her. The deals were just too enticing, despite the fact that she no longer needed the huge stockpiles that filled three freezers and an entire basement full of shelves. When the stockpile threatened to take over her house, she began including some of the stockpile in annual garage sales, as well as donating to a woman's shelter and allowing her adult children to "shop" in Mom's downstairs store.

Lisa's favorite store changes just as often as the deals do, but at the time of our interview even Lisa couldn't believe the amazing deals she'd been getting at Rite Aid. Combining sale prices, coupons, and the UP register rewards, Lisa once ended up with ninety-eight Johnson & Johnson baby products totally free. Besides keeping her own grandchildren well-stocked with baby products, she filled gift baskets for baby showers and church raffles with those deals.

RAYVEN

Rayven Perkins of North Virginia, has also been an avid couponer, off and on, since 2003. In her early thirties, Perkins is married to a man who literally and figuratively supports her desire to stay at home with their children. Rayven's website, www.stay-a-stay-at-home-mom.com, covers ways that mothers at home can make and save money, including couponing and bartering. Their family income of approximately $70,000 a year for a family of four allows her to indulge in some interesting hobbies, one of which is couponing. Perkin's interest in couponing mostly extends to the savings she finds on toiletries and health and beauty items, along with the deals she can find on healthy food for her family.

Years after the deal, Perkins still raves over a particularly exciting coup that she pulled off, repeating the same deal scenario over sixty times at Target, and filling a freezer full of meat while netting enough excess bags of charcoal that she was able to barter for a night at a whirlpool suite at a historic mansion bed and breakfast. She also bartered charcoal for a camping lamp, fishing poles and reels, and bicycles for the family. Her repetitive trips went something like this: add an 18-pound bag of charcoal to the cart, one jar of KC masterpiece Sauce, a Hormel pork roast, two pounds of ground beef, and three dollars in fresh produce. By strategically combining coupons good on Kingsford, free sauce when you buy charcoal, $6 off pork when you buy both charcoal and sauce, $4 off beef when you buy Kingsford, and a "$3 off" produce coupon when you buy Hormel roast, Rayven was able to walk out of the store having paid just $6.47 for $25.96 worth of food. Repeating that sixty times, she netted over fifteen hundred dollars worth of food and charcoal for less than four hundred dollars.

Not only does Perkins relish the deals like this that fill her own cupboards, she often donates surplus items to women's and homeless shelters. Her future project is a well–thought out plan of bartering for materials to build a house. Instead of using or selling a clinical strength deodorant that she got free with coupons, she has traded that same deodorant at the retail value of $7.99 for an equal amount in locally grown foods or other items. Initially, she traded through Craigslist and the Farmer's Market, but Perkins plans on an ultimate barter when she and her husband begin building on land they've purchased. They plan on building their own eclectic, mortgage-free, "recycled" home made entirely of previously owned, bartered, or freecycled materials and labor. Her skill with couponing will help them get there.

CHRISTINE

Christine of Long Island, New York, isn't alone in her coupon habit. Both she and her husband are avid coupon users. Financially, they don't *need* to be. Their combined household income exceeds $200,000 a year. Their house is completely paid off, and they own a vacation home and another investment property. Yet, thanks to prudent coupon use, they save over 75 percent on their weekly grocery bill. Not only that, but they have learned to always ask for a discount from merchants. Once, she got a hundred dollar discount for paying in cash at the dentist. Another time, it was a seven dollars a week discount on weekly landscaping.

"It doesn't seem like a lot, but that was a yearly savings of 168 dollars, just for asking," Christine told me. "That 168 dollars paid for our dinners out and summer piano lessons for my daughter."

"Although we don't need to use coupons, I can't imagine not using them. Why pay full price when you don't have to? The money we save sends our kids to expensive private school, summer camps, and helps us afford three major vacations a year."

RANDI

Randi Lehman, of Syosset, New York, is in her early fifties and has been using coupons for over twenty years, despite the fact that now she and her husband's combined income exceeds $500,000 a year. When she got married, her husband was just one year out of law school and money was tight. Her mother had always used coupons, so she decided to try it to save money. Grocery shopping became a game, seeing how much she could save each week using coupons. By the time her son was born, fifteen years ago, she discovered a website where she could trade coupons for products she used every day. With that trading opportunity, a new game began. Not only did she save money at the grocery store, but with the knowledge she gleaned from the website, she also discovered huge savings at the drugstores and even department stores. Now, her motivation is seeing how many products she can get for free or for pennies, specifically to donate to a food bank and women's shelter. Like Rayven Perkins, she has also discovered a way to profit off the excess good deals. She started a business that includes making custom decorated ladies bathroom toiletry baskets for Bar and Bat Mitzvah's and weddings. She uses coupon-purchased items like free nail polish and inexpensive or free sanitary napkins or tampons to fill her baskets.

CORI

Cori Nadler of Coral Springs, Florida, used to just dabble a bit in couponing until January 2011 when she realized she had to make a change in the amount of money her family of four was spending on food. At the time, they spent 150 to 200 dollars a week, and she wasn't even sure what they were buying. Her 2011 New Year's resolution was to save as much money as she could with coupons, and soon she was hooked. Couponing turned into a new career for her. When she began sharing deals on Facebook, her good deal alerts went viral and soon she started a fan page, "Cori's Coupon Corner." Formerly a teacher, it was only natural she started teaching couponing workshops.

"I love the thrill of winning at the savings game," Cori says, "My daughter plants herself at the end of the checkout lane so she can watch my total go down. She high fives me when it gets really low."

JOHN

It isn't just women who become avid couponers. John Hoerner, of Massachusetts, used coupons even as a single guy in 1975. Using coupons then gave him a little extra spending money. When he and his wife, Pauline, got married in 1979, it was a match made in Coupon Heaven. They both have been using coupons faithfully ever since. They even call their weekly shopping trips "treasure hunts."

John benefits from the fact that their Stop and Shop and Shaw's food stores double coupons. He also finds a lot of good deals at drug stores like Rite Aid and Walgreens. Because companies often promote their new products with high-value coupons and simultaneous sales, John loves being able to sample the new product for very little outlay of cash. John likes the idea of trying new products for very little outlay of cash when coupons and sales promote a new product. Besides stockpiling for their own household, John donates excess stockpiled items to a local food pantry. The couple tried selling some of their stockpiled items at a flea market for the first time in summer 2010 and found that staples, like aspirin and laundry soap, just flew off the table.

"I like the bond I've formed with employees at some the stores I regularly shop at," John comments. "Couponing has taught me to go the extra mile in being nice to the employees. They call me by my first name and greet me with a big smile."

DEREK

Derek Adler, thirty-four, is married and lives in Bridgewater, New Jersey. Derek and his wife are both scientists. Derek blames his Adult Attention Deficit Disorder (AADD) for his avid coupon use. The same disorder that allows him a hyper-focused attention to details in his work with a major pharmaceutical company gives him a decided advantage when it comes to couponing. After all, it is the strategic moves of combining sales prices with coupons that allow him to stockpile enough good deals to donate to the local food bank and two animal shelters.

Derek's used coupons for years, getting heavily involved since March 2009, when he discovered he could save over 90 percent on their grocery bill. That month, he'd lost his coupon folder in the same week their local A&P offered a triple coupon event. He went through their newspapers and cut out every single coupon 99 cents and under. With just those in hand he was still able to buy a hundred dollars worth of groceries for just under ten dollars. That did it. He was hooked on the super savings that can be had with coupons. Since then he cuts out every coupon, filing them in two thirty-three-page accordion folders.

He doesn't mind letting co-workers and friends know about his new coupon obsession because they will save their coupon inserts for him. He admits that while some of his friends might think he is nuts for couponing, they still like to hear how much he saved at the store that week.

Because of his couponing endeavors he, and his wife have enough deodorant, shampoo, toothpaste, peanut butter, and other non-perishables to last a full year or more—a stockpile that came in handy when he was temporarily unemployed last year. His biggest couponing feat was in 2011 when someone gave him hundreds of Huggies and Pampers peelie coupons. He posted his bounty on Facebook and ended up sharing batches of coupons to friends who could use them. Then he needed them himself. He and his wife had their first child in October 2011, and now their couponing centers on infant products.

Derek's money-saving ways extend further than just the coupon binder. He joined a Crop Sharing Association to enjoy locally-grown foods and to cut down on monthly costs for produce. His wife cans and jars fruits and vegetables to preserve or to give as gifts. Alongside their stockpiled cans from the grocery store are jars of peaches, apple butter, homemade relish, and more homegrown goodies. Derek is a strong believer in recycling and passing on the savings. Besides the local food bank and shelter, he has shared with family members and once brought dozens of free Gatorade to his wife's cousin's football team. Even the newspapers he pulls the inserts from get recycled when he brings them into the animal shelter for animal bedding.

PAUL

Paul Woods of Bald Head Island, North Carolina, started couponing in the 1980s while he attended college. He credits his father's sage advice to "always try to save money" for getting him started. Couponing fit fine into that philosophy. After college, he met his future wife on the Prodigy Interactive Service couponing bulletin board. They have four children and keep a stockpile of free and cheap products on the mainland. Because Paul is self-employed as a consumer consultant and his wife works full time as a hospital administrator, most of the coupon clipping is left to Paul and the kids.

Paul says the power shopping trips "jazz him up."

"It makes me feel empowered. I have all this free stuff, and I see people ahead of me paying two hundred dollars for their cart full of items, and I only pay ten dollars, most of which is tax."

Do these people sound like "crazy couponers" or just everyday smart shoppers who like to get the most for their hard-earned money? They might not typify the average shopper, but they are representative of the avid couponers I know.

The Bottom Line

This mostly-true spoof was published in the now-defunct "Refund Express" newsletter in 1996, shortly after I'd given birth to our sixth child. I used that same coupon box up until May of 2011. The station wagon is long gone. So are the jeans.

ROMANCE IN AISLE 3

She entered the store with a spring in her step, her first lone outing since the baby was born. She'd taken great care with her appearance. The daily walks had paid off, and she was finally able to get back into her jeans, albeit lying down on the bed to zip them up. The waistband cut painfully into her protruding belly and she winced every time she bent over, but didn't they say that beauty hurt? The baby was asleep, the sun was out, and she had one glorious hour in which to peruse the grocery store aisles before her husband left for work. Just the fact that she was dressed, in makeup, and out the door before 8:00 a.m. was a miracle in itself. But with her well-organized coupon box and grocery list in hand Mary felt as though she could conquer the world today. She felt the familiar rush of adrenaline as she approached the produce section. Bags of overripe bananas lined the shelves and were marked at 39¢ each. Two bags went into her cart.

It was in Aisle 1 that she noticed him. A young man was filling his cart from the display of Pepsi at the end of the aisle. As she walked by, Mary noticed him checking her out. It had been a long time since a man had looked at her in that way, other than her husband of course, and Mary couldn't help but feel flattered. She pretended not to notice him. He was barely twenty, if that, and had the sleek physique of a young man involved in contact sports. He reminded her of the blond guy on the Dukes of Hazzard show her oldest son used to watch.

By the time she'd gotten to Aisle 2, she realized she'd forgotten the cans of chunk chicken that were on sale and she had a coupon for, so she headed back to the previous aisle and ended up only inches away from the blonde Adonis who was chucking several cans of beef ravioli into his cart. Mary felt his eyes on her as she pulled three coupons from her coupon box and put the matching three cans of chicken in her cart. She realized that she also had several coupons in the box good on ravioli. Her children hated canned pasta, so with her heart beating wildly, she offered the man her four coupons to apply towards his purchase. He accepted them with a smile that could advertise any of the tooth-whitening toothpaste.

Mary headed for Aisle 3, noticing that the young man followed quickly behind her. Determined to show him that she was way more than just a pretty face, she carefully compared coupons to sale prices, dropping six boxes of the rice dishes she had coupons for into her cart. They would cost her just a few cents each. Mary's coupon fever rose as she briskly went from aisle to aisle, matching coupons to sale prices. By the time she reached the baby food aisle she'd almost forgotten the young man who was watching her.

"Well, there goes my cover," she thought as she put twelve jars of baby food (free with coupon) into her cart. "Now he knows I have a baby," her thoughts continued. "But surely he would never guess I have five older children."

It was at that moment she felt her jeans give in the front. Her zipper had just broken. She was grateful for the long shirt she'd worn, sure that no one could tell. She breathed a huge sigh of relief, the first good breath she'd taken since zipping them up. By the time she reached the cereal aisle, Mary was getting a little irritated that they young man still seemed to be following her. This was where she had planned a good coupon attack. Many cereals were on sale for $1.67 a box and she had dozens of 50¢ coupons. Her cart was already overflowing, and Mary was annoyed that other customers seemed to be staring. She was sure they were thinking that either she was a pig, or had an army to feed. At this point she would be relieved if the manager of the store announced that a mother of six was approaching the checkout.

Her face flushed, she juggled two boxes of cereal that fell off the cart and entered the checkout closest to the *doors. Sweating with the effort of pushing the overloaded cart, she felt her underarms perspiring heavily, probably staining her blouse. As she waited in line, Mary straightened her blouse over the open zipper of her jeans, brushed back her unruly hair, and noticed the young man in the cookie aisle, still watching her. As the total approached the hundred dollar mark, she wished the floor would open up and swallow her. She knew she only had eighty dollars left in checking. She handed the cashier the stack of coupons and watched the total dwindle until she could triumphantly write out a check of $72.89.*

While the stock boy loaded up the back of her station wagon, Mary noticed the young man heading her way. Her mind racing, she wondered how to let him down. She was happily married, the mother of six. If her ravishing beauty had given him pause, had made him fall in love with her at first sight, it wasn't her fault. She always wore her wedding ring, she'd bought baby food, she drove a station wagon, for goodness sakes! Mary looked straight into the young man's eyes as he approached, ready to defend her honor and her marriage, ready to break the young man's heart.

"Excuse me," he said, "I couldn't help but notice you in the store." Mary's direct gaze didn't waver, though her brain was rapidly trying to come up with a way to let him down easy.

"My mom is about your age. I was trying to come up with a perfect birthday gift for her and wondered where you got that great coupon box . . ."

I took great pride in "doing it all" during my years of avid couponing, including the well-organized shopping sprees that made me the local Coupon Queen. Even before beginning this book, I'd considered the fact that extreme couponing has been a part of my life for so long that I might have lost some objectivity regarding the intrinsic value of avid couponing and stockpiling.

An interesting thing happened as I was delving into the history of couponing and refunding, and interviewing other extreme couponers. I found myself abandoning some of my long-held couponing practices. I left my coupon binder at home more often and changed some of my own extreme shopping habits. I stopped purchasing coupons. I no longer traveled great distances for a single good deal, nor did I lament missing a Target "75% off" post-holiday sale. I could actually pass over some super deals without hyperventilating. The change was gradual, but my husband, my "deal-hunting partner" of over thirty years noticed. I didn't completely abandon my use of coupons, but it was an eye-opening experience to view myself through the lens of the very microscope I was directing at extreme couponers.

Just who are the extreme couponers? That is the question I asked when I began the book, hoping to have a specific profile of the avid couponer by the time I'd completed it. I shudder to think that viewers of the TLC's *Extreme Couponing* television program might believe they've viewed the typical couponer. The premiere episode featured four coupon-obsessed savers who were challenged to get as much merchandise as they could for as little as possible.

I should have known that a reality program would portray the extreme couponer in an unflattering light. Amanda was presented as a hoarder who had enough toilet paper in her stockpile to last her and her husband forty years. Despite his protests, her two rooms full of stockpiled groceries were spilling into a third room, her husband's "man cave." Nathan Engles, also known as "Mr. Coupon" online and among friends, had 1500 sticks of deodorant stockpiled in his garage. "The Krazy Coupon Lady," Joanie Diemer, was shown pilfering for coupons in a dumpster alongside her four-year-old son. Neither Nathan nor Joanie's regular donations to food banks was mentioned, though later programs would focus on some of the donations. Viewers would be bored with my minimal stockpiles, though my double coupon opportunities might have merited a few "oohs and ahhs" from someone who'd never experienced such a trip of their own. I know I impress some of my workshop attendees with the slides I show of those big hauls in my power point presentation.

The effect of the *Extreme Couponing* television program is widespread. When I do coupon workshops, I always begin my presentation by asking how many in the room have seen the program. After a show of hands, I ask how many want to shop like that. I am sure I disappoint a few in the room when I tell them it is virtually impossible to replicate those kinds of trips here in Iowa.

Would the participants in the reality show be the only image of extreme couponers this book's readers knew? Was this the image they would be familiar with: people who stockpiled three thousand rolls of toilet paper and fifteen hundred deodorants, outrageous amounts that they couldn't possibly use in their own lifetime? What grocery store manager would actually allow a customer to empty their shelves, fill nine grocery carts, and use nine hundred coupons in a single transaction, and still be smiling about it? None of the stores I shop at even stock those amounts of products.

And where was the coverage about the huge donations Nathan Engles regularly makes to a local church food bank? Or the information that Diemer teaches others to coupon through her book, *Pick Another Checkout Lane, Honey* and her website, www. KrazyCouponLady.com? Reality shows aren't most people's reality, but would the average television viewer know that? Was this the how majority of Americans would view extreme couponers?

During the months I conducted research and wrote this book, one of my sisters, briefly unemployed, joined the ranks of extreme couponers, netting me a cohort in the hunt for good deals. Then in November of 2010, a local Pamida store experimented with tripling coupons, allowing me the unexpected and unprecedented enjoyment of several triple-coupon sprees that filled Christmas baskets and my attic stairwell. Also that month, my mother died after a courageous battle with cancer. While cleaning out her closet, my sisters and a niece came across an unusually long, thin box. I gasped with amazed recognition when my niece opened it up and pulled out a delicate lavender umbrella with a swan head handle. It was an unopened premium from the Gloria Vanderbilt Company. For two empty flattened perfume boxes, they'd offered the lovely umbrella as a refund almost twenty years before. I'd had enough empty boxes in my files to have one sent to me and another to my mother. Here was definitive proof that she'd never even used it. I'll never know if she'd thought it too beautiful to use in the rain, or considered it worthless. Somehow it seemed appropriate that I discovered that past company premium while working on a book about coupons and refunding. Finding it abandoned in a closet made me wonder: Is "free" always a good deal? The free umbrella had done nothing for my mother, except take up valuable closet space.

If the TLC *Extreme Couponing* show and the discovery of the unused umbrella weren't enough to give me pause, I'd also began reading a book about hoarders and a description of their tendency to surround themselves with "stuff." This description of an avid "collector" is from that book, *Stuff: Compulsive Hoarding and the Meaning of Things* by Randy O. Frost & Gail Steketee:

> *The fantasies increase the object's subjective value and give it a magical quality, and soon the value of the object outstrips and becomes disconnected from any functional utility it may have. Next comes the hunt, frequently the most pleasurable part of collecting. Many collectors shift from a self-focused state to what some have described as a "flow state," a mental state in which the person is so absorbed in the activity that he or she is unaware of his or her surroundings—commonly experienced by an athlete at the height of physical exertion or by someone immersed in a game or project.*
>
> *Watching a passionate collector at a flea market makes it clear that his or her state of consciousness is altered during "the hunt." The person has little appreciation for anything going on around him or her; only the pursuit matters. When the acquisition occurs, it is accompanied by a wave of euphoria and appreciation of the object's*

features, which become part of the story of the acquisi-
tion. Finally, the excited collector catalogs the object and
adds it to the collection, arranging for its display. (Pages
54–55)

I felt a twinge of discomfort and a sense of recognition reading
these words. Replace the word "collector" with "couponer," and it
described my relationship with couponing in a nutshell. Each of
my children has heard my dismissive tone at least once when we
are in a store and I spot a special sale. "Just a minute, honey. I'm
in the zone," I've said in response to their urgent plea to go to the
bathroom, visit the toy aisle, or whatever need they have conveyed
to me at an inopportune time during my hunt for good deals. I've
avoided taking them with me to a book sale, consignment store
bag sale, or clearance sale precisely because of how I operate "in
the zone." I've definitely experienced the euphoria and have been
known to artfully arrange a display of my wares and snap a photo
to share with others. Yes, I am willing to concede that my obsession with coupons hasn't always been healthy or wise and that
the savings were sometimes only an illusion. There are times my
stockpiling has bordered on hoarding. Deal shopping could have
the potential of taking valuable time from something else in a person's life, like their husband, family, or other hobbies. I happened
to share my hobby with my husband and children, but did they
always enjoy it nearly as much as I did? Did the children have a
choice, or were they unwilling participants in some grand social
adventure that involved boxtops, labels, and hundreds of pieces of
paper their mother coveted more than purses and jewelry?

Is it also true that couponing, particularly double couponing, devalues a brand, as Jill Cataldo contends in an October 2012 CPGMatters report? If so, what can happen when a consumer accumulates a large stockpile of free items?

I need look no further than my bathroom cabinet and reflect back on the "bandage incident" to know the truth of devaluation. Several years ago, one of my children, a child who shall remain nameless, appeared before me as I worked at my desk. She was plastered head to toe with bandages. Rather than gasp in dismay at the waste, I admired her creativity in finding something that had apparently entertained her and a sibling for a good hour while I worked on submitting rebates. This was back in the day of plentiful refunding, when I could spend a good hour or two in my office, fulfilling offers. At the time, I'd stockpiled an entire shelf of bandages in my bathroom cupboard, bandages that had been completely free with coupons. Seeing a plentiful supply of the product, my enterprising children had orchestrated a session of "doctor"—a session that involved a badly injured patient needing bandages to stem the flow of imaginary blood. *Because the bandages were free,* I not only failed to correct my children on the proper use of bandages, I actually encouraged their play, with the use of additional bandages. It was only later, when I saw the carnage of empty boxes in my bathroom cupboard, that I questioned the advisability of allowing children to waste something just because it happened to be free. I emptied the remaining boxes into a container with a tight-fitting lid and put it out of the children's reach. But the fact remained; I had definitely devalued a product because it had been free. As I reflected on these things, I was uncomfortably aware that I had occasionally "crossed the line" in my couponing and stockpiling behavior.

In addition to these remembrances of years past, researching coupon fraud and conducting searches on the auction site eBay left a bad taste in my mouth. It became apparent that a dark underbelly of the coupon world exists, despite the best efforts of people like Bud Miller of the CIC and honest coupon advocates like Jill Cataldo.

As if all this insight and contemplation weren't enough, what

STORE COUPON

"People often don't care as much about things they don't pay for, and as a result, they don't think as much about how they consume them. Free can encourage gluttony, hoarding, thoughtless consumption, waste, guilt, and greed."

from *Free: The Future of a Radical Price*, by Chris Anderson

really changed my coupon hobby during the writing of this book was the unexpected death of my husband David, my coupon shopping buddy for thirty-two years, in March of 2012. For weeks afterwards, I didn't touch a coupon. I couldn't have cared less about shopping or couponing, despite my need to continue touting the hobby in my workshops and presentations. I couldn't even make it through a grocery store without breaking down in tears. While David hadn't been actively involved in the coupon end and never quite understood how I did my "coupon magic" to bring totals of over two hundred dollars down to less than twenty dollars, he was an eager and supportive companion on the majority of my shopping trips, my helping partner at the recycling bins where we'd collect extra coupon inserts in the early 1990s, and my biggest all-around cheerleader in both my couponing and writing endeavors. His pride in my shopping prowess never ceased to amaze, and sometimes, embarrass me. "Isn't she something?" he'd gush to the cashier at the final tally, slinging his arm around my shoulders affectionately, beaming from ear to ear.

Coupon inserts piled up for several months as I grieved the man who'd encouraged this very book. My priorities shifted dramatically. Who cared about bargain hunting or stockpiling in the face of a tremendous loss? For the first time in thirty years, I ran out of necessities. I had to go on an "emergency run" to the local discount store one evening, horrified to pay full price for feminine protection. Not once in thirty years had I run out of sanitary pads or toothbrushes, and my supply of both products were depleted during the same week.

I wrote this tribute to my husband for a now-defunct refunding bulletin, "Refund Express." Unfortunately, David and I never reached the age of the couple in my imaginary scenario, but ours was a true couponing love story:

ROMANCE AT EDGETON'S SANITATION

Our eyes met across the newspaper recycling bin as our hands brushed against each other's in our search for the glossy coupon inserts amidst the piles of newspapers. My heart beat faster and my cheeks flushed red with excitement. After fifteen years, this man knew the way to my heart. He smiled as he handed me a huge stack of uncut coupons, and smiling more broadly, he pulled a Motrin IB box from his coat pocket. "Look what I found in the cardboard bin," he said excitedly, "And I bet there is more where that came from."

Sound like a trashy romance novel to you? Write what you know, successful authors advise, and I know what it's like to have a husband who not only supports my hobby, but who also believes I'll have a book published by the time I reach forty. Most of us have some type of support system in the form of a spouse, a parent, a refunding sister, or our regular traders who visit us via the mailbox. If we are really lucky, we live with our supportive person. I'm one of those lucky enough to have a spouse who thinks refunding is both fun and profitable.

Pulling an old curtain rod from the back of his maroon station wagon, David deftly cornered a forty-two-load ultra detergent box in the cardboard bin, flipping it over the side with one twist of his muscular arm. My knees trembled and my heart raced as I saw him reach deep into the large bin for yet another treasure to warm my heart. Dimly I was aware of another car approaching the site. I busied myself unloading my own box of recyclables, keeping an eye on David, who continued to look through the cardboard-filled bin, oblivious to the well-dressed older couple who'd pulled up in their van.

There have been times in my life when I've actually been embarrassed by my relationship with trash. It helps to have a spouse who has offered to buy me a Halloween mask to conceal my identity for trash digs. David tells me that someday we will look back on these days and laugh, or I will write about our experiences and be invited to the Oprah show. Our children have seen the great gifts I get for Christmas morning, so they are well aware what refunding can do for them. Anyone who looks in my bathroom cupboard and sees the shampoo, toothbrushes, soap, and makeup that I've gotten practically free through the wise use of coupons is impressed. But my husband also sees the piles of undone refunds on my desk, the stacks of trades to be answered, the overflowing basket of labels and UPCs on my kitchen counter, and the huge box of qualifiers in my office/schoolroom. I can't pinpoint the exact day when my husband did more than just tolerate my hobby, but I do know that the arrival of the Camel/Salem camcorder in the mail did a lot to convince him of the value of refunding. A shopping spree where I paid $45 for over $295 worth of groceries didn't hurt either.

I couldn't resist checking out the magazine box, where I'd been caught by a worker at the site recently who encouraged me to take the magazines home. I love reading and can't always afford to pick up the latest women's magazines. Besides, I'd recently bartered ten Mother Earth News magazines I'd found for two books by an author who wrote about homeschooling. I noticed the couple in their van warily eyeing David before finally getting out and emptying their own boxes. I was pleased when they approached my bin with a bag of what looked like People magazines, a gold mine for me! I smiled at the woman as she dumped them, and she smiled back. I saw her speaking to her husband when she returned to the van and he nodded. I wondered if they were feeling sorry for the poor woman who had to get her reading material from a recycling bin. I caught David's eye and nodded to him that I was done for the day.

Together, David and I are learning what we can do without, what we really need, and all the fun stuff we can get for free. I like being thrifty with my husband and would love to get a government grant to study the effects of couponing and refunding on the average marriage. Surely someone who has seen you bent over digging through a recycling bin and has not only stayed with you, but joined in, must love you a great deal.

I took hold of David's hand as he started the car and leaned over to kiss me. "We got a good haul today," he said, glancing in the back at the boxes brimming with coupon inserts, magazines, and detergent boxes. He sighed with contentment as we drove out the entrance of the recycling center. I looked at him with appreciation, and then saw his face change from pleasure to that of surprise as he looked in the rearview mirror. He abruptly braked, then pointed back to the recycling center. "Look," he whispered. I turned to see the older couple facing each other across the same newspaper bin David and I had shared a tender moment at just minutes before. The woman was gesturing excitedly to her husband, waving a stray coupon insert in front of him. He laughed and caressed her cheek lovingly. I looked at David, and we didn't even need to voice the thought we were both having . . .

That's us, in twenty-five years.

After his death, I had to wonder: without David at my side, did I even want to continue couponing? Was it worth my time and the effort involved? When the *Extreme Couponing* producers contacted me in April of 2012 and suggested they cover my true couponing love story as a human interest feature, I began frantically stockpiling again, but I didn't enjoy it as much as I once had. When my son Matt moved out, our household consisted of just four females, hardly the size of family I'd always needed to stockpile for. I unplugged my basement freezer and filled totes full of peanut butter and cereal for the cupboards of my college son's first apartment.

Negatives aside, I have also seen how couponing can benefit one's own family, as well as others. As a stay-at-home mother of several children, I used coupons to stretch our thin budget. That feat gave me a great deal of satisfaction. My well-stocked cupboards had always been a source of pride for me, as have my Christmas gifts and baskets and the prize baskets I put together for my couponing workshops. I've also been able to donate to food banks and put together boxes of health and beauty items for families in need, when I might not have been able to otherwise. Presenting couponing workshops helped me see how much I enjoyed public speaking and teaching, second only to my love of writing. Couponing has been a huge part of my life, and I will always remain a deal seeker. I've gradually begun using coupons again, but not to the degree I used to.

Who exactly are the extreme couponers? Obviously, the answer isn't that easy. We can no more pigeonhole the avid couponer than we can the families that choose homeschooling. Saying that all homeschoolers are fundamentalist Christians turns out to be just as untrue as labeling extreme couponers as hoarders. Many of the couponers I spoke with didn't even have stockpiles, and some donated nearly everything they obtained free to charities. It turned out the only thing I could count on in my interviews was that love of talking about our shopping adventures. There are no hidden secrets to the method of our madness. The goal is the same: get the best values and pay as little as possible. Then, of course, there is the ultimate goal of getting something free. If companies haven't learned that simple lesson by now, then they could simply deduce it from the marketing mistakes of others.

Several years ago, the Sears Corporation distributed a "$5 off any purchase" coupon in the moving booklets available at post offices throughout the United States. When I heard about this amazing coupon, I immediately wondered, *What were they thinking?*, the "they" being the marketers behind such a concept. I knew what would happen as soon as the coupon community got wind of the offer, and I was right.

The intention of the coupon was one thing, the implementation of it yet another. While intended for use by the person picking up the moving booklet (*that is someone who was actually moving*) surely the Sears Corporation could have anticipated that there would be others picking up the moving booklets and using the coupons as well. What they hadn't taken into account was the group of people who would pick up more than one booklet, people like Grace J. of Colorado, who visited all of the post offices within a fifty-mile radius, picking up a dozen booklets in every town, clipping out the coupon, then driving to the nearby malls to search for a Sears store and hitting every checkout with coupon in hand. By the time the coupon expired, Grace estimates she got over three thousand dollars worth of underpants, socks, and clearance-priced merchandise totally free.

Grace was not alone. Even I, limited to one post office and one Sears store, managed to make enough visits before the coupon expired to net at least fifty dollars worth of free merchandise. Post offices resorted to hiding their booklets behind the counters, and Sears stores began limiting the amount of coupons that each household could redeem, while the corporate big-wigs in their offices shook their heads in dismay and asked, "What happened?"

What happened was *us*. The Sears Corporation didn't take into account extreme coupon users. The resulting fiasco could have been avoided in the first place if marketers understood the scope and influence of the select group of people that do not operate like the "average" consumer.

Fast forward to May 2009 when television talk-show host Oprah Winfrey announced that Kentucky Fried Chicken was offering a downloadable coupon good for two pieces of chicken, two side dishes, and a biscuit. More than ten million coupons were printed out. Overwhelmed KFC chains stopped honoring the coupon within forty-eight hours. Allegedly, about 5.7 million people were denied the free meal that otherwise retailed for $3.99. Lawsuits were filed, and a sit-in erupted in at least one KFC restaurant. While the company offered a rain check, it required customers to apply for their single meal via the Internet. That didn't placate a lot of unhappy and hungry consumers who not only wanted the free meal they were promised, they wanted free meals for their entire families and all their friends.

"I took my whole family out for a free dinner today," one couponer reported on a message board I frequented, "And I'm going to do it again tomorrow."

I could have warned the company what would happen when they distributed a downloadable coupon that could be printed multiple times. Even folks who wouldn't normally use a coupon couldn't pass up a free chicken dinner.

Craig Herket, chief executive at Supervalu Inc., operator of Jewel, Albertson's, and other supermarkets, said it best in a March 8, 2010, *Wall Street Journal* article about coupon clipping being the newest extreme sport. He told analysts that shoppers with an eye for discounts were "executing with surgical precision." Marketers using Groupon have noticed this as well. Social promotion users are not always the relational customers the businesses had hoped for when they signed up with Groupon. According to Rice University's Jones School of Business, a study of 150 businesses running Groupon promotions between June 2009 and August 2010 found that the coupon promotions were unprofitable

---

4632BN
12796

TAKE THIS COUPON TO YOUR STORE

10¢

In March 2008, Dr. Pepper offered a free can to everyone in America if Guns N' Roses put out its new album that year. The soft drink company probably thought it was safe to do so since the band had sixteen years of empty promises behind it. In November of that year, Guns N' Roses *Chinese Democracy* album appeared in stores. The overwhelming response to the Dr. Pepper offer crashed their website, and many were unable to download the free coupon. Dr. Pepper extended the offer online, adding a toll-free number to call. Guns N' Roses lawyer Alan Gutman labeled the campaign "an unmitigated disaster which defrauded customers."

10¢

12796

for 32 percent of the businesses that ran them. The businesses were disillusioned with the "extreme price sensitive nature and the transactional orientation of these consumers."

You mean, consumers like us, the extreme couponers? One respondent in the study noted: "Businesses need to consider that this class of consumers are bargain hunters. By nature they are frugal."

For those survey respondents who said their Groupon campaigns had not been profitable, only 25 percent of the redeemers of their offers spent more than the face value of the coupon, and only 13 percent came back a second time to shop full price.

Sorry guys, that is standard operating procedure for most of the couponers I know. We'll be happy to spend ten dollars on a forty-dollar value, but we're not going to spend more than that if we can help it, and we certainly aren't likely to come back and spend forty dollars for something we'd just gotten for ten dollars, unless it is something we desperately need and can't find elsewhere for less. And even then, we'd rather do without it than pay full price.

Marketers would do well to figure this out, because it looks like frugality is the new standard. According to an October 2009 online survey conducted by Booz & Company, a leading global management consulting firm, a "new frugality" was born of the Great Recession. Their survey of 2000 US consumers suggested that an increased frugality may have become learned behavior, making American consumers a more discerning type of consumer.

"Frugal behavior is now considered trendy by many shoppers, and will continue for years to come," said Matt Egol, a partner in Booz & Company.

Another study by Booz & Company in collaboration with Grocery Manufacturers Association, the *Shopper Marketing 3.0*, found shoppers conducting research before they shopped, with a focus on finding the best prices, clipping coupons, and reading circulars for what is on sale.

Results of "The 2010 American Pantry Study: The New Rules of the Shopping Game" concur. A joint project between Deloitte and Harrison Group was designed to quantify changes in consumer behavior and provide packaged-goods executives with an understanding of the new consumer. This study explored issues of post-recessionary purchasing resourcefulness and the impact on brands.

"We continue to witness consumers creating a whole new rule book and skill set for shopping that's based on value, not boasting of brands," said Pat Conroy, Deloitte's vice-chairman. "Our analysis concludes that personal gratification and a desire to feel smart about what consumers are putting in their shopping carts are trumping brand satisfaction, and that price-consciousness, value orientation, and bargain hunting will remain prevalent for years to come."

Even more telling, he continued, "This choice between brands heralds back to the consumer's belief that the game is not necessarily about the savings itself, but about the hunt for the savings and what goes into it—resourcefulness, planning, and precision. Consumers have become so skilled in executing their new approaches that most feel they have become smarter, more calculating shoppers. Moreover, this new 'badge of honor' will not fade away."

You've got that right, Mister. Avid couponers deserve a badge of honor. And that badge should come with a rebate, or at least a coupon for future purchases.

Wendy Liebmann, chief executive officer of WSL Strategic Retail, in a preview of its 2010 "How America Shops Mega Trends" study said it this way: "The Great Recession and how shoppers responded to it have fundamentally changed the future of retail."

Is all this another way to say marketers should be very afraid of the new breed of shopper, the frugal consumer? Not at all. Perhaps just a bit wary. They may need to tweak their marketing tactics a bit. Unless, of course, the lagging economy also increases the number of extreme "cherry pickers," which is not necessarily the same category as the "extreme couponer." The extreme "cherry picker" is the grocery store shopper who buys only sale items and nothing else. Cherry-pickers obtain 76 percent of potential savings at stores, stocking up on the negative profit items. Selling loss leaders is a necessary evil for grocery retailers since those sales help retain the existing customer base. The loss leaders at stores draw in the customers with the assumption that once inside the store, the customer will buy other items. Extreme cherry pickers, however, are more likely to come into the store only to load a cart with the sale merchandise, and then drive across town to do the same with a different sale item in another store.

On second thought, that does sound a lot like the extreme couponer.

In my own case, that is exactly what has happened when local stores experimented with double or even triple couponing. As soon as I got wind of an upcoming double coupon opportunity, I sorted through my coupon box for the highest-value coupons that might net a free product when doubled, whether I needed the item or not. If I was familiar with the store and the prices, I had a pretty good idea what coupons might result in free products. $1 off toothpaste? Check. $1 off deodorant? Maybe. $1 off Tylenol? Might not be free, but I go through a lot, and it could still be a good deal. Then I obtained as many coupons as I could from friends, family, and the coupon bin at the library. When there were limits on the amount of coupons each consumer could double, I brought my husband with me so I could have double the fun. And then I proceeded through the store aisles tossing those products that would be free or nearly free into my cart and matching those products up with the coupons from my carefully-organized box. By trip's end, I was leaving the store with a cartload of merchandise, upwards of 250 dollars worth, for less than 25 dollars. What the store was left with was empty spaces on their shelves and a register full of coupons that were worth half of the discount they gave me. Occasionally, I impulsively bought some items I didn't have a coupon for, but if the intention of the double coupon promotion was to get customers inside the store who would buy more than what they could get for cheap or for free with their coupons, then at least for me, their promotion failed miserably. Which makes one wonder why a store would continue to offer this kind of promotion? Unless, of course, only a few shoppers took advantage of the promotion to this degree, and the majority of consumers did, indeed, fill their carts with other supplies while they were inside the store.

That's exactly what happens, according to researchers Debabrata Talukdar and Dinesh K. Gauri. The results of their study were featured in a 2008 *Journal of Marketing Research*. Their research showed that only 1.2 percent of shoppers constitute the extreme "cherry pickers" and they only reduce profits less than one percent, suggesting that store managers who actually fear the cherry pickers are overestimating their effect on the bottom line profits. And if the results of recent studies are a reliable indicator of whether or not coupons are still a viable way for brand marketers to promote new products, then coupons are still a valuable marketing strategy.

In June of 2010, a social media marketing company called Syncapse looked at how valuable Facebook fans were to companies and estimated that someone who has "Liked" a brand will spend an average of $71.84 more each year on that brand's products or services than will someone who has not "Liked" it, for a total average annualized value of $136.38. Product spending was only one of the six fan benefits that Syncapse studied. The others were loyalty, propensity to recommend, brand affinity, media value, and acquisition cost. In most cases, the average fan was more valuable to the brand than the average non-fan.

Three Deep Marketing has worked with many well-known CPG brands that target moms. Their Google and BabyCenter

Mom's research supports these claims, indicating that using coupons for acquisition of new customers is a tactic that should continue to be used by CPG marketers. They found that seven out of ten moms will buy a brand at least twice after trying it with an online coupon. A 2000 study by Promotion Decisions found that advertising tended to produce twice the initial bump in sales it created, while trade promotions had little long-term multiplier

effect. Coupons, however, fell somewhere in-between, generating more repeat purchases than the trade promotion, but less than advertising.

So, have coupons become defunct in the fight to gain consumer's trust and their spending money? Not according to a pilot program at the C&K Market in Oregon. While digital coupons are all the rage, a so-called "retro-marketing" promotion at C&K Market in April of 2010 credits paper coupons for a double-digit increase in total store sales. One store even saw a 44 percent increase in sales from the year before. C&K operates sixty stores in Oregon and California. Their traditional marketing method involved a direct-mail booklet that contained thirty-two coupons. They were sent to loyalty cardholders at an Oregon store and five other hard-hit locations that seemed to be especially affected by the sluggish economy. Sales results showed that the coupons were achieving what C&K set out to do—build up its shopper base. While the stores are active on the Internet and social media, the success of the coupon booklet showed that the traditional paper coupon can still be effective in today's world.

From a marketing perspective, some things never change, and that means the mighty coupon will likely remain a valuable marketing tool. Ranging from their own store coupons to promotions like doubling manufacturer's coupons, retailers can view coupons as a weapon in their competitive arsenal. As for the consumer? It means they can combat the effect of high prices by learning to shop wisely.

Bare Bones Basics: Couponing 101

Remember my mistakes in the shopping game? Falling for the "blue light special" in Kmart and buying things I didn't need just because they are "on sale." This is one of the common mistakes made among consumers. I still make those kinds of mistakes, just not at a Kmart or with a blue light special. Having signed up for every deal site on the Internet has resulted in my inbox being inundated with daily offers. I have to be constantly vigilant. Just because Groupon offers me seventy dollars in stationery products for seventeen dollars, or Ebates doubles a store's cash back for a single day, doesn't mean I have to take advantage of those offers. I always have to ask myself if it was a purchase I would be making otherwise? Or would I just be spending money to take advantage of a perceived "good deal?"

This should have been the easiest chapter to write. For thirty-three years I've used coupons. I write a weekly newspaper column on couponing and present couponing workshops for community colleges and women's groups. I've even mentored a sister who began using coupons during the year I was writing this book. And yet, I dug in my heels and resisted writing this chapter—the how-to of the hobby. Why?

For one thing, there are entire books, websites, and seminars that can teach someone how to get started in couponing. My couponing workshops consist of a two-hour PowerPoint presentation with time for questions afterwards. The idea of teaching the same thing in a single chapter seemed daunting.

Then I remembered my own early couponing days, in an era when couponing automatically included refunding with its own set of tricks and rules. I learned the ropes by diving in and doing both. No one "taught" me how to coupon, though I certainly did learn from my peers in the couponing community. I reminded myself before beginning this chapter: couponing isn't rocket science.

I've divided this chapter into five main sections, and hope that even seasoned couponers will consider looking at the first two sections and reflect on the motives and time commitment of avid couponing.

- Motivation
- Time
- Organization
- Implementation
- Tricks of the trade

MOTIVATION

In chapter two we discussed motivational research. Before you take on the hobby of avid couponing, ask yourself why you want to use coupons. Is it because you want to fill entire rooms full of free products like the people you've seen on television? When I conduct couponing workshops, that is one of the first questions I ask, and I'm not surprised when half a dozen hands go up in the air. Do you want to experience, firsthand, the thrill of victory at beating the system when it comes to getting things totally free? Keep in mind that reality television isn't reality for most of us, but that doesn't mean we can't save money or obtain free items with our coupons.

Or, perhaps, is your interest in couponing more altruistic than that? Are you looking for a way to donate more to the local food pantry without breaking the budget? Would you love to make up inexpensive gift baskets with free health and beauty products?

Or is it as simple as you'd like to save some money on your grocery bill?

Maybe it just looks like a cool and fun thing to do?

Whatever your motives, the next step is to decide just how much time you want to involve in this new project.

TIME

Do you want to make this a full-time job, spending the majority of your waking hours online searching for deals, clipping coupons, organizing them, and then shopping at a half a dozen stores each week? This new endeavor can quickly become an obsession. All it takes is that one grocery cart filled to the brim with products that end up being free or nearly free after coupons, and you're hooked. And if you have access to double coupon stores in your area, then cartloads of free stuff is a very real possibility.

Would you prefer to have a life outside of couponing? Your husband and your children might have a say about the amount of time you put into couponing. In hindsight, gently lowering my toddler into an open recycling bin to retrieve stray coupon inserts, and trooping through alleys to tear off diaper box proofs of purchase might not have been the wisest or the healthiest choice for family activities when my children were very young. I don't think learning to compare prices and limiting cereal purchases to whatever was on sale with a coupon harmed them in any way, but there are limits to what your family can tolerate.

> Refunding and redeeming coupons yielded so many rewards for my family and me. I saved a lot of money using coupons at stores. By refunding, I received cash, stuffed animals, T-shirts, free food coupons, and many other wonderful products. So, it might be surprising to learn I no longer coupon. Yes, I still use the occasional one here and there, but I don't go at it big time like I used to. Why not? Well, simply put, life got busy. Suddenly, I didn't have the extra time to clip, file, and organize coupons. Nor did I have time to scour sales flyers in order to plan out grocery shopping trips. Someday, I'd love to get back into using coupons. I miss the thrill of the hunt for good deals and the feelings of satisfaction I received by saving all that money."
>
> TOWEL IS WORTH **25¢** OR MORE!
>
> Mary Jedlicka Humston, Iowa City, IA

You can certainly learn to save money with coupons but it is oh, so easy to become obsessed with it. I should know. I lived and breathed refunds and coupons for several years as a stay-at-home mother of several children. I was lucky to have a husband who not only tolerated, but encouraged my hobby. Always make sure your spouse is on board with any hobby that has the potential to take a great deal of your time.

ORGANIZATION

"I always cut out the coupons, but then I forget to use them." I can't tell you how many people make a similar comment when the subject of couponing comes up. This is a basic truth; you aren't going to use coupons at the store if you don't have them with you. It's as simple as that. Whatever amount of time you choose to spend at this hobby leads to the question of how you are going to organize your coupons. Are you going to be the woman in the grocery store who pulls out a crumpled coupon from her pocket, or are you going to carry two large binders full of neatly organized coupons everywhere you go? There are lots of in-between choices. I started out with two long white envelopes rubberbanded together: one for food coupons and another for the non-food. Women can stick these in their purse and men can keep the envelopes in the glove box of their vehicle. Most discount stores carry the small accordion-file style of coupon wallets for around a dollar. As you gather more coupons you might want a shoebox sized plastic bin with a lid. There are coupon organizers available online that do the majority of the organizing for you: plastic boxes with dividers already built in, some that fit in the baby seat of the shopping cart, and others that attach to the handle in some way. Do a search on

eBay for coupon organizer and you will see just how many different organizers there are. Which one should you choose?

In choosing an organizer, keep in mind your lifestyle and
motivation behind choosing this hobby. Are you disorganized
in every other area of your life? Then you might not want large
coupon keepers that require a lot of upkeep in organization. Do
you have small children that will be in the child seat of the grocery
cart? Your choice might be something you can hold onto, like a
coupon wallet, instead of something that takes up a great deal of
space in the cart. You can always upgrade as you get the hang of the
coupon hobby. Start with something small and work your way up
to a larger filing system. Make your choice work for you, and not
the other way around. I used a coupon wallet in my first year or two
of couponing, but quickly outgrew it and picked up a plastic check
file box with a hinged lid, at a garage sale. I labeled the dividers by
category. This worked perfectly fine for me for almost thirty years. I
dropped it once, lost it twice (but got it back—always include your
name and phone number inside somewhere). When the *Extreme
Couponing* show became popular, I noticed the women and men
in the show were always using a coupon binder. I had to admit the
coupon binders looked nicer than my beat-up old box. The prospect of changing over to a binder was pretty daunting, so until I
spotted a black briefcase style binder at a local thrift store, I'd had
no intention of ever changing over to one. Honestly, the thrift store
find was an impetus, but the fact was, after thirty years of couponing with a box of some sort, I was ready for a change. I liked
looking hip with a hobby that, until then, seemed anything but.

What I ended up doing was looking like everyone else. For thirty years I'd carried a coupon box with me everywhere and never saw another soul with one. Not one. I didn't see anyone with binders, either, but as soon as I changed from box to binder in May of 2011, I started seeing other "binder ladies" everywhere I went. Not only that, but in changing to a binder I made myself visible as a certain type of couponer, and unfortunately that backfired in some situations with cashiers who'd had it with "those coupon people." Alas, it was too much work to change back to the box, and I'd found I liked the binder better.

I won't go into detail about how to organize your coupons because you will have to find out what way works best for *you*. If you are new to the scene, you might want to check out some YouTube tutorial videos about organizing coupons. There are hundreds of videos, mostly in regards to organizing a binder. Keep in mind that you might want to start small with the coupon wallets that have been perfectly serviceable for eons.

IMPLEMENTATION

Now you've reached the "getting started" hurdle in the world of couponing. As my wise husband often reminded me, the toughest part of any job is getting started. Your first step was to find a way of organization. Of course, the second part of that is to locate the coupons you will be organizing.

In searching for coupons, some points to remember:

- The majority of coupons, nearly 90 percent, are still found in the Sunday newspaper coupon inserts.

- Magazines, such as *All You* are excellent sources for coupons.

- Tear pads and blinkie coupon machines on the stores shelves are another great source. Keep your eyes on the prizes you will find attached to shelves near the products or in the little red boxes (blinkies) that attach to shelves and spit out pertinent coupons.

- On-package coupons or peel-offs (peelies), attached to the bottle or package, are increasingly common and hard to miss.

- Store coupons are located right in the store's ads or online on their websites. Store coupons can usually be combined with manufacturer's coupons for maximized savings.

- Internet-printed, online coupons are available on sites such as Smartsource.com and Coupons.com

Returning to the subject of motivation and the science of shopping—when shopping either online or in the aisles of a brick and mortar store, always keep in mind that your goal is to save money and the store's goal is to see that you part with more of it. It's as simple as that. If you keep in mind that even the store's layout is designed for that purpose you can analyze your own shopping habits accordingly. Do you run to the store a couple of times a week just to get milk, only to end up spending forty dollars on things you hadn't intended on purchasing? These are the impulse buys stores count on, and you want to avoid them. Do you grab from the endcaps, assuming the sale price is a discount? Manufacturers pay for the prime spots and sometimes higher priced items are paired with the loss leaders. Don't shop blindly. Learn prices and comparison shop. Some couponers suggest making up a price book to keep track of average prices but I've found that as the primary shopper I pretty much know the average price of the products I purchase regularly. Do you shop mostly from the shelves at eye-level? Remember, lower shelves are not prime shelving. Lower shelves might mean lower prices.

Making a shopping list can just be an added chore to an already long to-do list, but anyone who wants to seriously lower their grocery bill should attempt one. The great thing about coupons is that they can actually make shopping less of a chore and more of a game: a game you can win if you plan your moves. Some general guidelines in shopping, which you may have heard a hundred times before, but that bear repeating:

Don't shop When you are hungry. It's funny how delicious that bag of chocolate-coated gourmet popcorn looks when you are ravenous, even though you'd never buy it otherwise. Impulse buys can be detrimental to both your waistline and your wallet.

Don't shop with your children. I inwardly cringe, giving that advice, since I was the mother with toddlers and babies in tow for so many years. I didn't have much choice, but if you do have a choice, choose not to bring your children. I once figured out that I spent an average of four dollars more on impulse buys when my children were with me, and when I was working so hard to save thirty dollars in each trip, that four dollars could have made it an extra sixteen-dollar savings each month.

If you have to take your children, involve them in your shopping. Even toddlers can play a match game, finding the product on the shelf that is pictured on the coupon. Make your shopping trips a real-life math lesson. Have your child tell you which package of gum is the better deal—the one priced at eighty-nine cents or the packages that are on sale three for two dollars. Allow one treat at the end of the shopping trip if they've behaved. I liked to reward my children with a twenty-five-cent lollipop if they didn't make me out to be the sucker on a shopping trip.

Use a grocery list. Research supports this. Having a list minimizes impulse buys. That said, I am going to go out on a limb and suggest that as a couponer, there are times when you shouldn't shop from your list. Once you get the hang of this hobby, you will be carrying your coupons with you everywhere you go: on vacations, on those quick "pick up the milk" trips, and even when you go out on a date with your husband. Why? Because sometimes the best deal in a store is an unadvertised one. It might be discounted diapers stacked up in a cart at the front of the store, or a clearance shelf located at the back. Seasoned couponers learn to take their coupons with them everywhere so that when they run across a cart full of diapers priced at four dollars a pack or deodorant marked down to one dollar, they can combine that dramatic savings with their coupons and get the products for *free*. That is when you should forget the list and snatch up products you weren't planning on purchasing that trip. Then, and only then, abandon your list and take advantage of the tremendous savings. Nearly half of my stockpile is items that came from clearance shelves or discounted carts—items I had not intended on purchasing but did anyway—because they were either free with my coupons, or cost just pennies. And we all know how quickly those pennies saved add up.

Watch out for impulse buys. This goes right along with having a list, but also includes those last-minute purchases encouraged while we are waiting in line. Pricey convenience items such as candy, mints, and interesting magazines are often located near the checkout stands, encouraging spur-of-the-moment purchases. The placement of merchandise is not left to chance. Makeup might be located near the women's shoes, high-priced salsa next to the sale-priced tortilla chips, or stuffed animals located at child's level precisely for the purpose of encouraging impulse buys

Beware the "paired" products. Be careful of store displays that pair up something expensive with the sale item on the shelves. Maybe the spaghetti on the endcap is the one-dollar sale price, but the sauce on the bottom shelf is the highest-priced sauce in the store.

Sneaky signs and sale prices. Don't let a sign dictate your purchases. Many sales (10 for $10) tempt the consumer to buy more of a product than they normally would. You usually don't have to buy ten to get the sale price of a dollar. Be careful. Sometimes the sale price isn't a good deal at all if the regular price is already one dollar.

Know your regular prices. I once got excited about a shampoo being on sale for $1, until I reached for it on the shelf and noticed the regular price was 97¢. In this case, the "sale" only meant that the company had paid a premium to be listed in an advertisement, not that there was a good deal to be had. And don't forget your elementary math lessons when looking at prices. $4.99 sounds like a great deal when compared to $5.00, but you are only saving one penny.

Compare unit prices. Check shelf tags below products to reveal the cost per ounce, quart, pound, or per hundred sheets. Bigger isn't always better, especially when you have a coupon to offset the price. Some couponers love getting free products so much that they will use their coupons that don't specify a size to get trial-size products free.

Know your store's official coupon policy. You may even want to go online and print it out, especially when an official policy changes. Cashiers might not be well trained in coupon acceptance and sometimes even a store manager is not aware of recent changes.

Register a separate e-mail address. Registering a separate email address just for your freebie and survey offers ensures that your regular email inbox isn't inundated with spam.

Write letters. Whether it is a letter of complaint or one of praise, write to companies either through the mail or via email. You can find their addresses on the side or back of the packages. Companies want to know how they are doing and will often send you high-value or even free product coupons in response.

Finally, be careful of the concept of a "good deal." "75% off" isn't a "good deal" if you don't need it.

TRICKS OF THE TRADE

Once you are organized, learn some tricks of the trade to really save money.

Pair store coupons with manufacturer's coupons. The majority of stores allow you to top off their own store coupon savings with your manufacturer coupons. Look at the top of the coupon in your store ad. Does it say "store coupon" or "manufacturer's coupon" next to the expiration date? If it says "manufacturer's coupon" then you can't use another manufacturer's coupon along with it, but if it is clearly labeled as a store coupon, you can combine the savings and really make out like a bandit, sometimes netting totally free products. If you are shopping at a store you've never been in before, don't just assume you can use two coupons— ask a manager. The cashier might tell you "no" even when the store's policy allows it, so it is best to ask at the customer service counter or request a manager's input.

Watch for sales when a coupon for a new product comes out. Frequently a manufacturer will introduce a new product with both a coupon blitz and sale prices to entice consumers to try their product. By watching the ads, a savvy couponer will wait for the sale to use the coupon, netting nearly free products. Not only that, but I've discovered that some of these new products will clearance out fairly quickly, either because the product idea didn't fly (anyone remember green ketchup?) or the original retail price was just too steep. I always clip the coupons for new products, keeping an eye on clearance shelves and carts for just that possibility.

Take advantage of catalina and register reward sales, and roll them. Drugstores like Walgreens, Rite Aid, and CVS may seem like an expensive place to buy your health and beauty items because their prices are so much higher than the discount stores of the world, but not if you watch the ads and take advantage of their sale prices and register reward deals. All of a sudden a $12.99 razor on sale for $9.99 with a $4.00 register reward is more appealing. If you use your $4.00 coupon on top of that, the expensive razor suddenly becomes a $1.99 bargain. The caution here is that you must remember to use the register rewards before they expire, usually within a two-week time frame. Also, in regards to the Walgreens register rewards, if you use a register reward for the same product, the registers are programmed not to give you another reward. So save your rewards to purchase something else. Some stores do allow you to "roll" the register rewards, meaning you can use the register rewards on the same item to get another reward. These rules, and even the form of store and register rewards are evolving rapidly as manufacturers try to figure out exactly what works in their favor, so ask a store manager if you are unsure of their policy.

Keep an eye out for clearance shelves. Some of your best deals will be the unadvertised, marked-down specials found on a clearance shelf or a grocery cart full of drastically-reduced merchandise. The code of conduct regarding leaving something for the next shopper totally flies out the window in this instance. If you have twenty coupons for "$1 off" a certain brand of toothbrush and there are twenty toothbrushes marked down to "$1 each," don't feel badly about taking them all. These toothbrushes weren't an advertised special that other customers were expecting to be on the shelf. If you know you truly won't use twenty tooth-brushes but that coupon is expiring in a few days, you essentially have three choices: buy them anyway and donate them to a food bank or shelter, be a "coupon fairy" and leave a few coupons near the marked-down brushes for the next delighted consumer to dis-cover, or pass over the deal entirely.

Price match. If you don't want to trek all over town to pick up the best deals, find a store that price matches and bring your ads in for one-stop shopping. Some stores will also accept competitor's coupons.

Keep an eye on the register. If you can't keep an eye on the cashier because you are busy attending to children or emptying the contents of your cart onto the conveyer belt, double check your receipt before you leave the store. You will want to make sure all your coupons were taken off and the sale prices rang up correctly.

Always remember couponing etiquette. Be polite and patient. You are never entitled to the coupon savings, and store managers do not have to accept coupons. Coupons are a privilege, not a right. You are doing yourself no favors if you enter stores with an attitude of entitlement just because you've been watching the crazy couponers on television!

And, finally, don't forget the cardinal rule of couponing: if you miss out on a great deal, don't fret and fume. There will always be another sale.

References and Resources

Rather than using formal footnotes and distracting from the text of my book, I've attempted to incorporate as many sources as possible—books, publications, websites, and studies—into the main text. Below are the chapter-by-chapter references related to academic and scientific studies cited throughout this book, followed by suggested resources for further study.

CHAPTER ONE

Hoffman, David. *Breakfast Cereal Gourmet*. Kansas City, MO: Andrews McMeel Publishing, 2005.

CHAPTER TWO

Ames, Lynne. "The View From Peekskill: Tending the Flame of a Motivator," *The New York Times*, August 2, 1998.

Anderson, Chris. *Free: The Future of a Radical Price*, New York: Hyperion, 2009.

Byron, Ellen. "A Virtual View of the Store Aisle," *The Wall Street Journal*, October 3, 2007.

Casimir, Jon. *The Gruen Transfer*, Lowfield Heath, UK: ABC Books, 2010.

Eden-Harris, Janet. "Study: Grocery Shopper Highly Susceptible to In-Store Marketing," *Retail Customer Experience*, June 6, 2010, http://www.retailcustomerexperience.com/article/21794/Study-Grocery-shoppers-highly-susceptible-to-in-store-marketing.

Eisenberg, Lee. *Shoptimism*, New York: Free Press, 2009. Gallagher, Julie. "Food Lion Cameras Track Shoppers in Two Test Stores," *Supermarket News*, March 23, 2010, http://supermarketnews.com/latest-news/food-lion-cameras-track-shoppers-two-test-stores.

Horovitz, Bruce. "Marketers Zooming In on Your Daily Routines," *USA Today*, April 30, 2007, http://usatoday30.usatoday.com/educate/college/business/articles/20070506.htm.

Kozinets, Robert V. "Motivation Research." In *Wiley International Encyclopedia of Marketing*, 1–8. Hoboken, NJ: Wiley, 2010.

Othmer, James P. *Ad Land: Searching for the Meaning of Life on a Branded Planet*, New York: Anchor Books, 2010.

Packard, Vance. *The Hidden Persuaders*, Brooklyn, NY: Ig Publishing, 2007.

Parker, George. *The Ubiquitous Persuaders*, North Charleston, SC: Booksurge, LLC, 2009.

Sheth, Jagdish and Naresh Malhotra. *Wiley International Encyclopedia of Marketing*, Wiley Publishing, 2010.

Tischler, Linda. "Every Move You Make," *FastCompany*, December 19, 2007, http://www.fastcompany.com/48949/every-move-you-make.

Underhill, Paco. *Why We Buy: The Science of Shopping*, New York: Simon & Schuster, 2008.

Vaczek, David and Richard Sale. "100 Years of Promotion," *Promo*, August 1, 1998, http://www.chiefmarketer.com/special-reports-chief-marketer/100-years-of-promotion-01081998.

CHAPTER THREE

Ailawadi, Kusum L., Donald R. Lehmann, and Scott A. Neslin. "Market Response to a Major Policy Change in the Marketing Mix: Learning from Procter & Gamble's Value Pricing Strategy," *Journal of Marketing* 65, no. 1 (2001):44–61.

Avery, Rosemary J. and George W. Haynes. "Estimation of Consumer Savings From Coupon Redemption," *Journal of Managerial Issues* 8, no. 4 (1996):405–424.

Berfield, Susan with Sapna Maheshwari. "JC Penney vs. The Bargain Hunters," *Bloomberg Businessweek*, May 28–June 3, 2012.

Brady, Diane. "Ron Johnson on the Progress of His J.C. Penney Remake," *BusinessWeek*, August 9, 2012, http://www.businessweek.com/articles/2012-08-09/ron-johnson-on-the-progress-of-his-j-dot-c-dot-penney-remake.

Brown, Charlie. "2012 Mid-Year Coupon Facts: Some CPG Marketers Hit the Brakes on Redemption, Giving Competitors an Opportunity," *The Coupon Sentinel: NCH Marketing Resource Center*, Special Edition, http://www2.nchmarketing.com/ResourceCenter/assets/0/22/32/112/196/266/e16ff07bf40d-4135b45e5ea72a13e8e9.pdf.

Clifford, Stephanie. "Knowing Cost, the Customer Sets the Price," *New York Times*, March 27, 2012.

Conte, Christian. "Stein Mart Reducing Coupon Use, Lowering Prices," *Orlando Business Journal*, March 8, 2012, http://www.bizjournals.com/orlando/news/2012/03/08/stein-mart-reducing-coupon-use.html.

D'Innocenzio, Anne. "JC Penney Reports Another Massive Loss in 4Q," *Yahoo! News*, February 27, 2013, http://news.yahoo.com/jc-penney-reports-another-massive-000916832.html.

Donovan, John and Maggie Burbank. "We Use Coupons: 'Super Couponers' Clip Their Way to Savings." *ABC News*, March 25, 2010, http://abcnews.go.com/Nightline/super-couponers-clip-savings-grocery-store/story?id=10198247#.UbFZOBJ-OVU.

Grant, Jack. "Redemption Soars as CPG Marketers Modify Offers to Balance Consumer Demand," *CPGMatters*, May 2012, www.cpgmatters.com/coupons0512.html.

Heller, Laura. "Ron Johnson Out At J.C. Penney, Ending Its Year of Living Dangerously," *Forbes*, April 8, 2013, http://www.forbes.com/sites/lauraheller/2013/04/08/wow-ron-johnson-out-at-j-c-penney/.

Hoffman, David. *Breakfast Cereal Gourmet*. Kansas City, MO: Andrews McMeel Publishing, 2005.

Inmar. "Consumer Coupon Usage statistics," *Inmar*, November 11, 2009, https://www.inmar.com/Pages/InmarArticle/Consumer-Coupon-Usage.aspx.

Jopson, Barney. "JC Penney Loses One-Third of Its Sales," *Financial Times*, February 27, 2013, http://www.ft.com/intl/cms/s/0/6b7ea8b4-8126-11e2-9fae-00144feabdc0.html#axzz2V-GacyrYh.

Leggatt, Helen. "Mobile Coupon Use Set to Soar," *Biz Report: Ecommerce*, July 26, 2010, http://www.bizreport.com.

Lyons, Daniel. "Click and Save," *Newsweek*, November 29, 2010, 25.

Market Tools. "Discount Hunters Reshaping the Grocery Shopping Experience," *Market Tools*, April 12, 2012, http://www.markettools.com/company/news-events/press-releases/discount-hunters-reshaping-grocery-shopping-experience.

Price, Gregory. "Cereal Sales Soggy Despite Price Cuts and Reduced Couponing," *Food Review* 23, no. 2 (2000):21.

Reichblum, Charles. *Strange and Fascinating Facts About Famous Brands*, New York: Black Dog & Leventhal, 2004.

Rueter, Thad. "Consumers Searching High and Low for Online Coupons," *InternetRetailer*, April 19, 2011, http://www.internetretailer.com/2011/04/19/consumers-search-high-and-low-online-coupons.

Wagstaff, Keith. "JC Penney Fires Ron Johnson: What Now?" *The Week*, April 9, 2013, http://theweek.com/article/index/242463/jc-penney-fires-ron-johnson-what-now.

Walker, Andrea K. "Coupons Keep Luring Customers," *Baltimore Sun*, June 17, 2007.

"The Great Coupon Caper," *Grocery Headquarters*, June 1, 1997, http://www.highbeam.com/doc/1G1-57479808.html.

"Stein Mart, Inc. Reports September 2012 Sales," *NASDAQ*, Oct 4, 2012, http://ir.steinmart.com/releasedetail.cfm?ReleaseID=711168.

CHAPTER FOUR

Arends, Brett. "Doing the Math on Coupons," *Wall Street Journal*, February 9, 2010.

Argo, Jennifer J. and Kelley J. Main. "Stigma by Association in Coupon Redemption: Looking Cheap Because of Others," *Journal of Consumer Research* 35, no. 4 (2008):559–571.

Brumbaugh, Anne and José Antonio Rosa. "Perceived Discrimination, Cashier Metaperceptions, Embarrassment, and Confidence as Influencers of Coupon Use: An Ethnoracial-Socioeconomic Analysis," *Journal of Retailing* 85, no. 3 (2009):347–362.

Calonia, Jennifer. "The Psychology of a Cheapskate: Can You Be Addicted to Saving Money?" *GoBankingRates.com*, October 24, 2012, http://www.gobankingrates.com/savings-account/cheapskate-psychology-addicted-to-saving-money/.

Coupons.com. "Coupons.com Names Top Frugalebrities," *Coupons.com*, February 1, 2012, http://www.couponsinc.com/corporate/OurCompany/PressReleases/2012.aspx?udt_619_param_detail=308.

Fox, Edward J. and Stephen J. Hoch. "Cherry-Picking," *Journal of Marketing* 69, no. 1 (2005):46–62.

Patel, Kunur. "Marketers Beware the Coupon Mom," *Advertising Age*, July 10, 2011, http://adage.com/article/special-report-couponing/marketers-beware-coupon-mom/228640/.

CHAPTER FIVE

Abramowitz, Rachel. "Disney Loses Its Appetite for Happy Meal Tie-Ins," *Chicago Tribune*, May 9, 2006, http://www.chicagotribune.com/topic/zap-disneymcdonaldsendhappy-meals,0,3643009.story.

Brean, Herbert. "The Box-Top Industry," *Life*, March 14, 1949: 127–132.

Freeman, William M. "Buyers at '63 Premium Show Find Yo-Yos and Mink Stoles," *New York Times*, September 10, 1963.

Johannes, Amy. "Disney, Nickelodeon Push Healthy Eating," *Promo*, October 18, 2006, http://www.chiefmarketer.com/promotional-marketing/sponsorshipstie-ins/disney-nickelodeon-push-healthy-eating-18102006.

Medney, Cliff. "Nutritional Standards," *Promo*, September 1, 2008, http://www.promomagazine.com/opinions/0901-ftc-kids-pledge/index.html.

Nagle, James J. "Trading Stamps: A Long History," *New York Times*, December 26, 1971.

Rich, Mark. *Warman's 101 Greatest Baby Boomer Toys*, Iola, WI: KP Books, 2005.

Taylor, Rod. "Fish Tale," *Promo*, June 1, 2005.

Taylor, Rod. "Peddling Premium Paddling," *Promo*, June 1, 2005, http://www.chiefmarketer.com/special-reports-chief-mar-keter/peddling-premium-paddling-01062004.

Vaczek, David and Richard Sale. "100 Years of Promotion," *Promo*, August 1, 1998, http://www.chiefmarketer.com/special-re-ports-chief-marketer/100-years-of-promotion-01081998.

"House Unit Scans Trading Stamps," *New York Times*, October 10, 1957.

"Trading Stamps: A Hidden Change in the Grocery Bill," *Time*, November 28, 1955, http://www.time.com/time/magazine/article/0,9171,861709,00.html.

CHAPTER SIX

Angrison, Carol. "Internet Coupons Again Subject of Contro-versy," *Supermarket News*, September 3, 2008, http://super-marketnews.com/latest-news/internet-coupons-again-sub-ject-controversy.

Beck, Koa. "The Feminine Marketing Mystique," *Customer Rela-tionship Management*, April 2011:18–22.

Johannes, Amy. "Online Coupon Posting Called Into Question," *Promo*, September 4, 2008.

Kanner, Bernice. *Pocketbook Power: How to Reach the Hearts and Minds of Today's Most Coveted Consumers-Women*, Berkshire, UK: McGraw-Hill, 2004.

Kraus, Steve. "Affluents, Coupons, and the Implications of a Female-Driven Marketplace," *MediaPost*, February, 15, 2012, http://www.mediapost.com/publications/article/167702/affluents-coupons-and-the-implications-of-a-fema.html#ax-zz2VGmtn1DD.

McNeil, Cheryl Pearson. "Power Moms," *New Pittsburgh Courier* May 5, 2010, http://www.newpittsburghcourieronline.com/index.php/business/1977-power-moms.

PRWeb. "The Digital Mom: Reaching the Internet's Most Influential Demographic," *PRWeb Newswire*, June 29, 2010, http://www.prweb.com/releases/Fuor-Digital/Digital-Mom/prweb4192704.htm.

Sauer, Jeff. "4 Things You Didn't Know About Mom," *CPG Blog*, February 16, 2010, http://google-cpg.blogspot.com/2010/02/4-things-you-didnt-know-about-mom.html.

"Big Fuel Study Reveals Secrets to Influencing Moms through Social Media," *Marketing Weekly News*, May 8, 2010, www.verticalnews.com/premium_newsletters/Marketing-Weekly-News/2010-05-08/4359AM.html

"Online and Connected: Women Are Leaders on Social Media, Blogs," *Marketing to Women: Addressing Women and Women's Sensibilities*, July 1, 2010, http://www.highbeam.com/doc/1G1-232179214.html.

"Social Media Moms: The Most Effective Ways for Marketers to Reach This Tech-Savvy Group," *Marketing to Women: Addressing Women and Women's Sensibilities*, March 1, 2010, http://www.highbeam.com/doc/1G1-221413498.html.

CHAPTER SEVEN

Alaimo, Dan. "New Technologies Deter Coupon Fraud at the Point-of-Sale," *CPGMatters*, August 2012, http://www.cpg-matters.com/Coupons0812.html.

Anderson, David. "8 Indicted Here in Coupon Fraud," *New York Times*, July 1, 1964.

Cosco, Joseph. "Grocery Coupon Scam Uncovered By Police," *Sun Sentinel*, March 13, 1986.

Coupon Maven [pseud.]. "Confirmed: 200 More Counterfeit Coupons Used on Extreme Couponing," *Jill Cataldo's Super-Couponing*, March 17, 2012, http://www.jillcataldo.com/extreme-couponing_counterfeittidecoupons.

Coupon Maven [pseud.]. "Couponing Ethics: Is It Wrong to Buy and Sell Coupons?" *Jill Cataldo's Super-Couponing*, February 29, 2012, http://www.jillcataldo.com/ethics_buyingand-sellingofcoupons.

Dalton, Richard. "Counterfeit Coupons Flooding the Supermarkets," *Tribune Business News*, December 30, 2003.

Harris, Art. "Coupon Connie, Clipped in the Bud: A Hot Shopper's Free Ride Ends at Prison," *Washington Post*, May 2, 1990.

Holt, Karen. "Coupon Crimes," *Promo*, April 1, 2004, http://www.chiefmarketer.com/special-reports-chief-marketer/coupon-crimes-01042004.

Jorden, Jay. "Verdict Clips Avid Coupon Collector in $2 Million Scam," *Chicago Sun-Times*, January 30, 1990.

Kesmodel, David. "The Coupon King," *Wall Street Journal*, February 16, 2008.

Martin, Timothy W. and Ilan Brat. "Coupon Fraud Grows," *Wall Street Journal*, March 4, 2010.

Mullins, Richard. "Tampa Tribune: The High-Stakes Game of Saving," *Jill Cataldo's Super-Couponing*, April 29, 2012, http://www.jillcataldo.com/coupon_tampa.

Soble, Ronald L. "Coupons Used by Creative Crooks," *Los Angeles Times*, March 21, 1988.

Taylor, Rod. "Cleans Away Dirt and Crime," *Promo*, April 1, 2006, http://www.chiefmarketer.com/special-reports-chief-marketer/cleans-away-dirt-and-crime-01042006.

Tuttle, Brad. "The $40 Million Counterfeit Coupon Caper," *Time*, July 19, 2012, http://business.time.com/2012/07/19/the-40-million-counterfeit-coupon-caper/.

"Food Coupon Fraud to Be Fought Here," *The New York Times*, August 27, 1951.

CHAPTER EIGHT

Calvey, Mark. "Refund Offers Can Add up to Savings—or Abuse," *Atlanta Journal and Constitution*, October 12, 1987.

Gibson, Richard. "Pious Town Finds Mighty Temptation in Coupon Clipping," *Wall Street Journal*, February 26, 1992.

Keeney, Irene Gardner. "Rebate Raiders Postal Inspectors Hunt Cheaters," *Albany Times Union*, March 30, 1989.

Rochell, Anne. "Woman Indicted in Rebate Scheme," *Atlantic Journal and Constitution*, April 7, 1993.

Sloane, Martin. "Supermarket Shopper," *Gainesville Sun*, December 9, 1993.

CHAPTER NINE

Angwin, Julia and Tom McGinty. "Sites Feed Personal Details to New Tracking Industry," *Wall Street Journal*, July 30, 2010.

Clifford, Stephanie. "Online Coupons Can Tell Stores More Than You Realize," by Stephanie Clifford, *New York Times*, April 16, 2010.

Clifford, Stephanie. "Web Coupons Know Lots About You, and They Tell," *New York Times*, April 16, 2010.

Everett-Haynes, La Monica. "Impending Death for Paper Coupons?" *University of Arizona News*, September 30, 2010.

Garry, Michael. "The DataBar Takes Over," *Supermarket News*, January 10, 2011, http://supermarketnews.com/technology/databar-takes-over.

Goldman, Sharon M. "An Offer You Can't Refuse: Today's Coupons are Becoming Paperless, Portable, and More Personalized," *AdWeek*, June 24, 2012, http://www.adweek.com/sa-article/offer-you-cant-refuse-141289.

Harnick, Chris. "6B in Revenue for Mobile Coupons by 2014: Juniper Research," *Mobile Commerce Daily*, November 4, 2009, http://www.mobilecommercedaily.com/6b-in-revenue-for-mobile-coupons-by-2014-juniper-research.

Johannes, Amy. "Online Coupon Posting Called Into Question," *Promo*, September 4, 2008.

Lyons, Daniel. "Click and Save: Coupons? Who'd Have Thought?" *Newsweek*, November 29, 2010:25.

O'Dell, Jolie. "The History of Groupon," *Forbes*, January 7, 2011, http://www.forbes.com/sites/mashable/2011/01/07/the-history-of-groupon/.

Oreskovic, Alexei. "Facebook Jumps Into Crowded Coupon Market," *Reuters*, April 27, 2011, http://www.reuters.com/article/2011/04/26/us-facebook-deals-idUS-TRE73P6GS20110426.

Prosser, Faye. "Thursday Thoughts: Couponing Study Shows Interesting Trends," *WRAL.com*, September 13, 2013, http://www.wral.com/5onyourside/smartshopper/blogpost/11543119/.

Saponto, Bill. "The Groupon Clipper," *Time*, February 10, 2011, http://www.time.com/time/magazine/article/0,9171,2048311,00.html.

Steiner, Christopher. "Meet the Fastest Growing Company Ever," *Forbes*, August 30, 2010.

Stross, Randall. "Someday Store Coupons May Tap You on the Shoulder," *New York Times*, December 25, 2010.

Walsh, Mark. "Coupons.com Hits $1 Billion in Redemption Value in First Half of 2010," *Media Post News*, July 26, 2010, http://www.mediapost.com/publications/article/132604/#axzz2VGmtn1DD.

"Nearly One-Third of Coupon Users Consider Themselves Opportunists When It Comes to Savings, Finds National Coupon Month Survey From CouponCabin," *MarketWatch* August 30, 2012, http://www.marketwatch.com/story/nearly-one-third-of-coupon-users-consider-themselves-opportunists-when-it-comes-to-savings-finds-national-coupon-month-survey-from-couponcabin-2012-08-30.

"What They Know," *Wall Street Journal*, 2010.

CHAPTER TEN

Angrisani, Carol. "C&K: Paper Coupons Drive Lift," *Supermarket News*, April 26, 2010, http://supermarketnews.com/market-ing/ck-paper-coupons-drive-lift.

Antil, John H. "Couponing as a Promotional Tool; Consumers Do Benefit," *Journal of Consumer Affairs* 19, no. 2 (1985):316–327.

Glionna, John M. "The Paper Chase: From Store Counter Back Home to Manufacturer, Your Coupons Travel Labyrinthine Route through 2 Countries, Countless Hands.," *Los Angeles Times*, November 8, 1992.

Kolodinsky, Jane. "Money-off Coupons and the Consumer: Are They Worth the Effort?" *International Journal of Consumer Studies* 16, no. 4, (1992):389–398.

Neff, Jack. "Coupons Get Clipped," *Advertising Age*, November 5, 2001, http://adage.com/article/news/coupons-clipped/53364/.

Uhl, J. N. "Cents-Off Coupons: Boon or Boondoggel for Consum-ers?" *Journal of Consumer Affairs* 16, no. 1 (1982):161–165.

"Top 10 Coupon Sites," *ShopSmart magazine*, May 2011, 32–37.

CHAPTER TWELVE: THE BOTTOM LINE

Anderson, Chris. *Free: The Future of a Radical Price*, New York: Hyperion, 2009.

Angrisani, Carol. "The Social Network," *Supermarket News*, November 8, 2010, http://supermarketnews.com/marketing/social-network.

Angwin, Julia and Tom McGinty. "Sites Feed Personal Details to New Tracking Industry," *Wall Street Journal*, July 30, 2010.

Fox, Edward J. and Stephen J. Hoch. "Cherry-Picking," *Journal of Marketing* 69, no. 1 (2005):46–62.

Gauri, Dinesh K., K Sudhir, and Debabrata Talukdar. "The Temporal and Spatial Dimernsions of Price Search Insights from Matching Household Survey and Purchase Data," *Journal of Marketing Research* 45, no. 2, (2008):226–240.

Ghosen, Jacqueline. "Grocery Retailers Need Not Fear 'Cherry Pickers,'" *University of Buffalo News Center*, September 19, 2007, www.buffalo.edu/news/releases/2007/09/8848.html.

Karolefski, John. "Do CPG Brands Welcome the Decline of Double Coupons?" *CPGMatters*, October 2012, http://www.cpg-matters.com/Coupons1012.html.

Mahoney, Sarah. "Deloitte Study: Consumers Love Spending Less," *Marketing Daily*, July 13, 2010, http://www.mediapost.com/publications/article/131827/deloitte-study-consumers-love-spending-less.html#axzz2VGmtn1DD.

Martin, Timothy W. "Hard Times Turn Coupon Clipping Into the Newest Extreme Sport," *Wall Street Journal*, March 8, 2010.

Neff, Jack. "Coupons are Hot, But Are They a Bargain for Brands?" *Advertising Age*, July 10, 2011, http://adage.com/article/special-report-couponing/coupons-hot-a-bargain-brands/228611/.

Quinton, Brian. "Groupon Social Coupons Unprofitable for One-Third of Marketers: Study," *Promo*, October 20, 2010, http://www.chiefmarketer.com/promotional-marketing/incentives/groupon-social-coupons-unprofitable-for-one-third-of-marketers-study-20102010.

Additional Suggested Resources:

BOOKS

Be Centsable, by Chrissy Pate and Kristen McKee, Plume, 2010.

Born to Buy, by Juliet B. Schor, 2004.

Brandwashed: Tricks Companies Use to Manipulate Our Minds and Persuade Us to Buy, by Martin Lindstrom, 2011.

Buy.ology: Truth and Lies About Why We Buy, by Martin Lindstrom, 2008.

Complete Idiot's Guide to Couponing, by Rachel Singer Gordon, 2012.

Consumer Behavior for Dummies, By Laura Lake, 2009.

Coupon Mom's Guide to Cutting Your Grocery Bills in Half, by Stephanie Nelson, 2009.

Cut Your Grocery Bill in Half, by Steve and Annette Economides, 2010.

The Everything Couponing Book: Clip Your Way to Incredible Savings, by Karen Wilmes, 2012.

Free Prize Inside: How to Make a Purple Cow, by Seth Godin, 2004.

How to Shop For Free, by Kathy Spencer, 2010.

The Lazy Couponer: How to Save $25,000 Per Year in Just 45 Minutes Per Week With No stockpiling, No Item Tracking and No Sales Chasing, by Jamie Chase, 2011.

The Money Saving Mom's Budget: Slash Your Spending, Pay Down Your Debt, Streamline Your Life, and Save Thousands a Year, by Crystal Paine, 2012.

Phil Lempert's Supermarket Shopping and Value Guide, by Phil Lembert, 2011.

Pick Another Checkout Lane, Honey, by Joanie Demer and Heather Wheeler, 2009.

Poplorica, by Martin Smith and Partick J. Kiger, 2004.

Saving Savvy: Savvy and Easy Ways to Cut Your Spending in Half and Raise Your Standard of Living . . . and Giving, by Kelly Hancock, 2011.

Spree: A Cultural History of Shopping, by Pamela Klaffke, 2003.

Strange and Fascinating Facts About Famous Brands, by Charles Reichblum, 2004.

What She's Not Telling You: Why Women Hide the Whole Truth and What Marketers Can Do About It, by Mary Lou Quinlan, 2009.

Why We Buy: The Science of Shopping, by Paco Underhill, 2008.

MAGAZINES

AdWeek: (www.adweek.com) Print and online magazine that delivers insightful content that appeals to the advertising, media, and marketing professionals.

Advertising Age: (adage.com) Print, digital, and online. Latest on advertising and marketing.

Chief Marketer: (www.chiefmarketer.com) Print and online. Covers all the best in measureable marketing. Includes an area of emphasis: PROMO articles.

Journal of Consumer Psychology: Publishes articles that contribute both theoreticaly and empirically to an understanding of psychological processes underlying consumer's thoughts, feelings, decisions and behaviors.

Journal of Consumer Research: Publishes scholarly research that descirbes and explains consumer behavior.

Journal of Marketing: Premier, broad-based, scholarly journal of the marketing discipline, focuses on substantive issues in marketing and marketing management.

ShopSmart: (http://www.shopsmartmag.org) Consumer Reports, market research, and ratings for consumers.

WEBSITES

Couponblender.com: The best deals from dozens of coupon sites.

Coupon Information Corporation (CIC): (www.couponinforma-tioncenter.com) Provides resources to prevent coupon fraud.

CouponIntegrity.com: Supports ethical couponing, lists blogs, and websites that promote ethical couponing

CouponNetwork.com: printable coupons

Coupons.com: Printable grocery coupon website. Their website also contains press releases and coupon-related news.

Ebates.com: Register and go through this site to earn money back on online purchases.

HotCouponWorld.com: coupon forum, database, online deals

www.jillcataldo.com: Super-Couponing blog, with coupon match-ups, the latest on couponing in the news.

www.nchmarketing.com: NCH, a Valassis company, is the global leader in business solutions for the redemption, settlement, and analysis of promotional offers. Includes coupon facts, fundamentals, and pertinent news and articles in the *Coupon Sentinel* newsletter

www.pgesaver.com: Load Procter & Gamble coupons directly onto your store loyalty card, and get news on their products.

Refundcents.com: Website of America's coupon queen, Michele Easter. Includes deals, forums, and information for saving money with couponing.

ShopatHome.com: Shop through this website for cash back on purchases at participating stores.

Smartsource.com: printable coupons

Supermarketguru.com: Phil Lempert, expert analyst on consumer behavior, marketing, trends, new products, and the changing retail landscape. Learn to shop smarter, eat healthier, and live better.

SUGGESTED BLOGS

There are thousands of blogs you could follow in regards to marketing, coupon news, and frugal living. These are the blogs and websites I've found most helpful. If you are searching for other websites, you can always click on the blogrolls of some of these websites to check out their recommendations.

Coupons in the News: (couponsinthenews.com) One of my favorite websites to keep up to date on what is going on in the world of couponing. Does an excellent job of compiling the latest news on the couponing forefront, with a wry sense of humor. Highly recommended. Check out his Facebook page www.facebook.com/CouponsInTheNews.

DanAriely.com: Dan Ariely does research in behavioral economics, author of *The Honest Truth About Dishonesty.*

Hip2Save.com: Coupon and deal saving website started by Collin Morgan, mother of three and proud wife of a former Marine, in 2008, to help others save money and live frugally in a hip and fun way. Highly recommended.

Iheartcvs.com: Covers deals to be had at CVS stores.

TheKrazyCouponLady.com: Teaches how to collect and redeem coupons with precision, includes a blog and deals for home, family, style and finance.

MoneySavingMom.com: An upbeat and encouraging blog from Crystal Paine, blog dedicated to finding good deals, stretching your dollars, and living on less so you can save more and give more.

SethGodin.com: Seth has written fourteen bestselling books on marketing and leadership. *American Way* magazine calls him "America's Greatest Marketer."

stay-a-stay-at-home-mom.com: Rayven Perkins runs this jam-packed website full of deals, tips, and ideas for mothers who want to live frugally and save and make money.

TotallyTarget.com: Resources to help you save money at Target. (Not affiliated with Target.)

FREE APPS FOR YOUR PHONE FOR COUPONING AND DEAL-HUNTING

These are some of the free applications for your phone;

Amazon Mobile: Good for comparing prices to see if you can get something cheaper online. Free app that lets you compare prices, read reviews, and make purchases on Amazon.com.

Bizrate: Browse department store-style, comparing items and prices.

CardStar: For organizing all your loyalty cards in one app, also gets you in-store discounts.

Cellfire: Type in your zip code, select the coupons you want to use and enter your loyalty card information for a particular store and the coupons are saved directly to your card. When you give the card to the cashier, the savings are deducted from your bill instantly.

CouponCabin: Has loads of online coupon codes.

Coupon Sherpa: Hundreds of coupons available for dozens of stores. Cashiers can scan them directly from your phone.

Foursquare: "Check in" to stores when you shop there, for instant discounts and free samples.

Grocery IQ: A mobile app for your phone, owned by Coupons.com. Build your shopping list by scanning bar codes, find free coupons for items, and print coupons or have them added to your store loyalty card.

Nextag Shopping: Search for online retailer with the best discount.

RedLaser: Barcode app that allows you to scan barcodes on products and search for low online and local prices.

RetailMeNot Coupons: Search for coupons.

SavingStar: Website that is also available as an app for the Apple and Android devices. Has digital coupons for more than 24,000 supermarkets and drugstores around the county. Instead of saving at the cash register, the money is added to your Saving-Star account. You can opt for a cash payout, an Amazon gift card, or a donation to American Forests.

Shooger: Finds local and national coupons for stores you trust. Use coupons immediately or "clip" them for later use.

Shopkick: Earn points just for entering participating stores. Cash them in for free merchandise and restaurant meals.

Yowza!!: Finds coupons for stores in your area and sends them to your phone for the cashier to scan.

About the Author

It all started innocently enough in 1969, when ten-year-old Mary Potter Kenyon spied an offer for a free Super Ball on the back of a Cheerios cereal box. Before long, she was clipping the Sunday coupons and foraging in her mother's cabinets for labels to send in for cash. When she started her own family in 1980, Mary Potter Kenyon began honing her couponing skills to become a local Coupon Queen.

Mary graduated from the University of Northern Iowa with a BA in Psychology. She lives in Manchester, Iowa, with three of her eight children. Mary currently writes a weekly couponing column for the *Dubuque Telegraph Herald*, where she is touted as the "Tri-State Area's Coupon Queen." She holds couponing and writing workshops for NICC and Hawkeye, area community colleges, writing workshops at the River Lights bookstore in Dubuque and does public speaking for women's groups, libraries and writing conferences.

In addition to her career as a couponer, Mary has worked as a freelance writer for twenty years and has had over three hundred articles and essays about parenting, saving money, and homeschooling published in newspapers and magazines such as *Home Education, The Sun, Backwoods Home, Back Home, The Writer, Woman's World,* and the online magazine *LiteraryMama.com*. Her essays have been featured in seventeen anthologies, including five *Chicken Soup* books. An essay of hers was featured in the January/February issue of *Poet & Writer's* magazine.

About Familius

Welcome to a place where mothers are celebrated, not compared. Where heart is at the center of our families, and family at the center of our homes. Where boo boos are still kissed, cake beaters are still licked, and mistakes are still okay. Welcome to a place where books— and family—are beautiful. Familius: a book publisher dedicated to helping families be happy.

Familius was founded in 2012 with the intent to align the founders' love of publishing and family with the digital publishing renaissance which occurred simultaneously with the Great Recession. The founders believe that the traditional family is the basic unit of society, and that a society is only as strong as the families that create it. Familius's mission is to help families be happy. We invite you to participate with us in strengthening your family by being part of the Familius family. Go to www.familius.com to subscribe and receive information about our books, articles, and videos.

Website: www.familius.com
Facebook: www.facebook.com/paterfamilius
Twitter: @familiustalk, @paterfamilius1
Pinterest: www.pinterest.com/familius

CPSIA information can be obtained at www.ICGtesting.com
Printed in the USA
BVOW072045130613

323275BV00002B/12/P